The Vision of Emerson

Richard Geldard received a Ph.D. in Classics from Stanford University, an M.A. in English from the Bredloaf School of English at Middlebury College, and a van Horn fellowship to Oxford University in 1985 where he researched his first book (*The Traveler's Guide to Ancient Greece*). From 1970 to 1987 he held administrative positions and taught English in secondary schools. He currently teaches philosophy at Yeshiva University in New York City. He is also the author of *The Esoteric Emerson* (1993).

The Spirit of Philosophy Series

"This series of books offers the core teachings of the world's greatest philosophers, considered for the light their writings throw on the moral and material crises of our time. Repositioned in this way, philosophy and the great philosophers may once again serve humankind's eternal and ever-new need to understand who we are, why we are here, and how we are to live."

Jacob Needleman, Ph.D.
Series Editor

In the same series

The Vision of Kant by David Appelbaum
The Vision of Wittgenstein by Henry Le Roy Finch

THE SPIRIT OF PHILOSOPHY SERIES

The Vision
of Emerson

Introduced and edited by
Richard Geldard

ELEMENT
Rockport, Massachusetts ● Shaftesbury, Dorset
Brisbane, Queensland

To my Emerson students past, present, and future

Copyright © 1995 by Richard Geldard

First published in the USA in 1995 by
Element Books, Inc.
42 Broadway, Rockport, MA 01966

Published in Great Britain in 1995 by
Element Books Limited
Shaftesbury, Dorset SP7 8BP

Published in Australia in 1995 by
Element Books Limited for
Jacaranda Wiley Limited
33 Park Road, Milton, Brisbane 4064

Cover design by Max Fairbrother

Designed and typeset by Linda Reed and Joss Nizan

Printed and bound by Biddles Ltd,
Guildford and King's Lynn

British Library Cataloguing in Publication data available

Library of Congress Cataloging in Publication data available

ISBN 1-85230-626-2

10 9 8 7 6 5 4 3 2 1

CONTENTS

PART ONE
General Introduction

Emerson: Philosopher and Seer

In school texts Emerson is referred to as a transcendentalist and his movement Transcendentalism. The words suggest well enough a doctrine opposing materialism and emphasizing intuitive and spiritual values, but do not accurately describe Emerson's life or work. He called his vision Idealism and said about it,

> What is popularly called Transcendentalism among us, is Idealism; Idealism as it appears in 1842. As thinkers, mankind have ever divided into two sects, Materialists and Idealists; the first class founding on experience, the second on consciousness; the first class beginning to think from the data of the senses, the second class perceive that the senses are not final, and say, the senses give us representations of things, but what are the things themselves, they cannot tell. The materialist insists on facts, on history, on the force of circumstances, and the animal wants of man; the idealist on the power of Thought and of Will, on inspiration, on miracle, on individual culture. ("The Transcendentalist")

In our own time, the difference between materialism and idealism expresses itself in sense-based definitions of reality on the one hand and mind-based or conscious-ness theories on the other. The materialist depends on what the senses (and their instruments) report as facts and then develops knowledge systems on those reports. The idealist does not accept the reports of the senses as final or absolute in the search for truth or reality. If reali-ty is defined as "the actual nature or constitution of things," the materialist will see one set of characteristics to define "the nature" of things, and the idealist another.

In philosophy, then, the nature of the manifest world has always been the burning issue. For Plato, ulti-mate reality was the Idea behind the manifestation, the Idea being an actual entity. For Aristotle, who eventually parted ways with his mentor Plato, reality was the essence of the thing, essence also being substantial but not an actual entity. For Emerson, the nature of reality was a realm entered through consciousness.

> This open channel to the highest life is the first and last reality, so subtle, so quiet, yet so tenacious, that although I have never expressed the truth, and although I have never heard the expression of it from any other, I know the whole truth is here for me. What if I cannot answer your questions? I am not pained that I cannot frame a reply to the ques-tion, What is the operation we call Providence? There lies the unspoken thing, present, omnipresent. Every time we converse, we seek to translate it into speech, but whether we hit or whether we miss, we have the fact. ("New England Reformers")

The subtle space between Idealism and conscious-ness is the crucial interval in Emerson's grasp of reality.

For him, mind was the proper organ for the study of reality. He said in "Self-Reliance," "Nothing at last is sacred but the integrity of your own mind." Although more will be said about this seminal statement, suffice it here that for Emerson mind is the basis of all human contact with the realms of higher consciousness and is the means by which we experience divinity.

The term "idealism" appeared at the close of the seventeenth century to describe Platonism and the theories of archetypal Ideas. The term gained wide acceptance in philosophical circles when Kant used it to describe his own theory of knowledge. Emerson is often connected to Kant for this reason, but Idealism for Emerson has more ancient roots and derives from doctrines of Gnostic thought going back to Orphism, Heraclitus and his Logos, and before that to Eastern doctrines as expressed in the Vedas. Emerson took what he called the "lustres" from these ancient doctrines and made them his own. Emerson's theories of consciousness rest on his experience of the mind as a continuum of functions including vital functions, understanding, intellect, and reason, which is the point of contact with the Over-Soul, or Universal Mind, and by extension to the Divine Mind and on to the One or Absolute. In this continuum, consciousness in one of its higher forms created the cosmos. What we see and experience as nature is the result of the actions of this consciousness. Emerson believed that this same creative power is latent in human beings, but nonetheless always present. He called this power Instinct and experienced it as the revelations of the soul in the human mind.

Instinct and Reason Come Together

To the idealist instinct is a broad-reaching, inclusive power. Emerson said that the first instinct is the child's attraction to the breast.

> The Instinct begins at this low point, at the surface of the earth, and works for the necessities of the human being; then ascends step by step to suggestions which are when expressed the intellectual and moral laws. ("Natural History of the Intellect")

In an earlier lecture ("School") Emerson said, "Instinct, in the high sense, is so much our teacher as to exclude all other teaching, but its means and weapons are the secondary instincts, the wants and faculties that belong to our organization."

In the chapter of *Nature* entitled "Idealism," Emerson made the connection between Coleridge's use of the term Reason and his own use of Instinct.

> When the eye of Reason opens, to outline and surface are at once added, grace and expression. These proceed from imagination and affection, and abate somewhat of the angular distinctness of objects. If the Reason be stimulated to more earnest vision, outlines and surfaces become transparent, and are no longer seen; causes and spirits are seen through them. The best moments of life are these delicious awakenings of the higher powers, and the reverential withdrawing of nature before its God.

The distinction which Emerson makes about the nature of the world and the senses is that our true business lies in clearing away the impediments in the mind that perceives these layers of opaque matter with which the world appears to be constructed, so that we see through to an ultimate reality. An intuitive reasoning is the instrument of that penetration. The experience of transparency, those "delicious awakenings," may be rare in human experience, but they are the basis of Idealism. Emerson's purpose was always to convince us that we are organized in such a way as to be able to experience these fruitful moments of perception.

The idealist sees this organization of the human being in very expansive terms; the materialist sees it not at all. Ideally, we are organized to perceive a wide range of impressions, from the lowest impulses of touch and smell to the highest intuitions of moral law and divine revelation. That materialists deny revelation is a function of their reductive definition of human nature. What the senses do not report, they say, cannot, therefore, exist.

Emerson's Vision of Human Nature

Every true philosopher must eventually lay out a vision of human nature, one which answers our crucial questions: Who are we? What is the meaning of our existence? How are we to live? The idealist reaches into *a priori* definitions of human possibility and relationship to divinity derived from ancient sources and confirmed by the intuition as revelation. Emerson was always very careful about the nature of revelation, saying that emanations from the Eternal One or Over-Soul were never personal. All revelation is therefore related to principle and to the laws that govern the universe.

Much of the articulation from eighteenth- and nineteenth-century thinkers about Idealism may seem to us now extravagant or romantic. To hardened realists in a post-modern world where values are nonexistent or, at best, relativistic, Idealism may seem relegated to the ash heaps of outworn thought. In Emerson, however, Idealism was wedded to a tough, radical New England stance with no room for sentimentalism or fuzzy thinking. It has a touch of granite in it, something like the huge rough-hewn boulder that marks his grave in the Sleepy Hollow Cemetery in Concord.

The beauty of Emersonian Idealism is that nothing we are capable of experiencing is left out of its circle. The grace of a bird in flight draws our eye to its perfection. The idea of the bird appears and draws our mind to its essence and to the consciousness which creates it. Our sense of wonder in the presence of its perfection opens the channel of feeling to the dynamic laws that allow the bird to soar and to the laws that permit a circle of language to close around its existence and open out its nature. The momentariness of such action is identical with our perception of it. Such unity prepares us for new, personal steps in the same direction.

Emerson applied an ancient Idealism to the rigors of his own Puritan past and then to the demands of his New England present. The results are both practical and inspiring. Indeed, in Emerson's hands, Idealism is the only practical philosophy because it transcends tragedy and gives us the means to prevail in the face of life's blows. Anything else leaves us without the means both to know the nature of the day and to face it with magnanimity.

A Transcendent Vision

When Emerson was sixteen and a junior at Harvard, he began keeping a journal. Journal-keeping, at least of the sort Emerson maintained for nearly half a century, is one of the major philosophical tools. Using the gift of language, we have developed writing (sentences, para-graphs, essays) as a tool to formalize the capacity of thought. Writing is the microscope and telescope of thought, letting us see and then record the smallest and most cosmic of perceptions.

From a philosophical point of view, the journal is a record of the examined life. As Emerson developed the discipline over the first four years of observation, he used its pages as a mirror to see himself in the light of possi-ble futures and to record his adolescent longings for companionship and personal greatness.

The journals have naturally been the source of much analysis, partly because they reveal more of the personal Emerson than do the essays, playing to a banal, but nonetheless appealing, curiosity. Most critics assume that this more revealing material signals a mind more restless and doubting than we find in the formal work. If, how-ever, we take the journals for what they were meant to be (the accurate record of thoughts and feelings arising in his mind), then we see them as Emerson's process of distancing himself from those negative qualities he felt would inhibit his development. Giving doubt or longing formal expression means that an aspect of mind—called, for example, the Observer—has taken note of a mood or a fanciful reaction to another person or event. Seeing the thought and then writing it down releases us from the hold the thought might have on us. It is a way of dissolv-ing illusions.

A philosopher keeps an accurate record of his thought the way a bank records transactions. Without a record of thought, the serious thinker has no way of measuring his wealth or of examining a point of view retrospectively. One indication of the success of Emerson's journal-keeping is the sheer volume of material involved. After half a century, Emerson amassed at least 179 regular journals and numerous smaller note and account books, making a total of 230. Some did not survive, but the bulk did, and they now reside safely in the Houghton Library at Harvard University, where they are available to scholars.

A second indication of the success of the journals was the extent to which Emerson mined them for essay and lecture material. The Harvard University Press editions of the *Journals and Miscellaneous Notebooks* indicate each instance of Emerson's use of an entry in his published work. He employed a vertical mark through a passage to indicate to himself when he had used the material. It is instructive to see how material changed from journal to essay, sometimes to preserve his own and others' privacy and sometimes to sharpen the ideas for the benefit of his audience.

In December of 1823, when Emerson was twenty and had been keeping his journal for four years, he recorded a perception stimulated by Archimedes' famous dictum, "Give me a place to stand on and I will move the earth." From a philosophical standpoint, a place to stand, outside the self, where we can observe with an objective eye, is a powerful fulcrum in the world of thought. The significance for Emerson of this new stance was reflected in the journal entries which followed. They reveal a new confidence as well as a higher level of objectivity. There is, in fact, a new voice.

The journal Wide World 12 is entitled "A Place to Stand" (in the Greek) and contains the following powerful affirmation:

> Who is he that shall control me? Why may not I act & speak & think with entire freedom? What am I to

the universe, or, the Universe, what is it to me? Who
hath forged the chains of Wrong & Right, of Opinion
and Custom? And must I wear them? Is society my
anointed King? Or is there any mightier community
or any man or more than man, whose slave I am? I
am solitary in the vast society of beings; I consort
with no species; I indulge no sympathies. I see the
world, human, brute & inanimate nature; I am in the
midst of them, but not *of* them; I hear the sound of
the storm,—the Winds & warring Elements sweep
by me—but they mix not with my being. I see cities
& nations & witness passions,—the roar of their
laughter,—but I partake it not;—the yell of their
grief,—it touches no chord in me; their fellowships
& fashions, lusts and virtues, the words & deeds
they call glory and shame,—I disclaim them all. I say
to the Universe, Mighty one! thou art not my mother;
Return to chaos, if thou wilt, I shall still exist. I live.
If I owe my being, it is to a destiny greater than
thine. Star by Star, world by world, system by system
shall be crushed,—but I shall live. Dec. 21.— (JMN,
II, 190)

Such extraordinary detachment for a twenty-year
old! Emerson had found his place to stand, and it was
not a psychological indifference to the world but rather a
philosophical stance which recognized an aspect of his
(and our) nature that remained eternally still within the
turmoil of experience. "I live," he wrote, and in that
assertion proclaimed his idealism. Here was the outline
of the work. A lifetime of study and reflection filled in
the details.

A life-enhancing philosophy grows out of the
thinker's own experience, not from the pages of a book

or the perceptions of others. What the young Emerson gleaned from Archimedes and what he wrote down in his journal had to find correspondences in his own experience in order to appear with such power as language. Experiences which have the force to shape a whole life occur only rarely. For Emerson, such experiences were dutifully recorded in his journal and often developed in his published work.

The Transparent Eye

The "transparent eyeball" experience is one such famous example of a personal revelation evolving into a vision of human nature and a philosophy of life. The published passage appears in *Nature*. The original journal entry for 19 March 1835 reads,

> As I walked in the woods I felt what I often feel that nothing can befall me in life, no calamity, no disgrace, (leaving me my eyes) to which Nature will not offer a sweet consolation. Standing on the bare ground with my head bathed by the blithe air, & uplifted into infinite space, I become happy in my universal relations. The name of the nearest friend sounds then foreign & accidental. I am the heir of uncontained beauty & power. And if then I walk with a companion, he should speak from his Reason to my Reason; that is, both from God. To be brothers, to be acquaintances, master or servant, is then a trifle too insignificant for remembrance. O keep this humor, (which in this lifetime may not come to you twice,) as the apple of your eye. Set a lamp before it in your memory which shall never be extinguished. . . . I ought to have said in my wood-thoughts just

now, that there the mind integrates itself again. The attention which had been distracted into parts, is reunited, reinsphered. The whole of Nature address-es itself to the whole man. We are reassured. It is more than medicine. It is health. (JMN, V, 18)

Emerson did not use a term like "reinsphered" in his formal writing, but here in the journals it is a provocative way to describe the effect of this experience on his mind. The impression in his mind in relation to nature was experienced as an integration, a making whole or a com-pletion of the globe of human and natural history. It was an occurrence of self-recovery.

Between the observation as recorded in the journal and the subsequent rendering of the passage in *Nature*, a process of shaping occurred, a waiting for words to express the universal nature of the moment. Here is how the passage found its way into print.

Crossing a bare common, in snow puddles, at twi-light, under a clouded sky, without having in my thoughts any occurrence of special good fortune, I have enjoyed a perfect exhilaration. I am glad to the brink of fear. In the woods too, a man casts off his years, as the snake his slough, and at what period soever of life, is always a child. In the woods, is per-petual youth. Within these plantations of God, a decorum and sanctity reign, a perennial festival is dressed, and the guest sees not how he should tire of them in a thousand years. In the woods, we return to reason and faith. There I feel that nothing can befall me in life,—no disgrace, no calamity, (leaving me my eyes,) which nature cannot repair. Standing on the bare ground,—my head bathed by the blithe air, and uplifted into infinite space,—all mean egotism vanishes. I become a transparent eye-ball; I am nothing; I see all; the currents of the Universal Being circulate through me; I am part or particle of God. The name of the nearest friend sounds then foreign and accidental: to be brothers, to be acquaintances,—master or servant, is than a trifle and a disturbance. I am the lover of uncontained and immortal beauty.

The differences between the journal entries and what finally appears in print demonstrate the nature of philosophizing. It is the dialectic, what Emerson defined as driving through a subject to its essence. In moments such as this the veil of ordinary sense perception is lifted and we see. Although we cannot share the same perception as Emerson merely through his description of it, we can take from his language an essence which serves as a guide. It is like a map of the sublime landscape, which if we are ever fortunate enough to visit can validate our own experience.

The One and the Two

A wit once said, "There are two kinds of people in the world: those who divide things into twos, and those who don't." In the Western tradition, the dualists are in the majority. In the East, "those who don't," that is, those who see and exist in the essential unity in things, may still rule. In "Plato, or the Philosopher," Emerson described the tension of these two views in these terms:

Philosophy is the account which the human mind gives to itself of the constitution of the world. Two cardinal facts lie forever at the base; the one, and the two.—1. Unity, or Identity; and, 2. Variety. We unite all things by perceiving the law which pervades them; by perceiving the superficial differences, and the profound resemblances. But every mental act,—this very perception of identity or oneness, recognizes the difference of things. Oneness and otherness. It is impossible to speak, or to think, without embracing both.

Perception of the law is what allows us to see behind or beneath variety to the unity of things. In our mental experience we seek the unity behind the diversity of thought in an attempt to resolve the tensions of duality, the separation between our thoughts and our actions, the separation we feel as individuals seeking to merge our experience to the fact of the cosmos.

Since Plato, philosophy has been primarily the struggle to penetrate the illusory world of things through to reality. For Plato the absolute truth was perceived through the exercise of the dialectic, a penetration of illusion through dialogue: the Socratic method. The struggle between dualism and unity in philosophy finally ended with Descartes and the victory of dualism. Only God himself could mediate between the mind/body split. Human beings had lost control. We were then modern, a radically divided self with no hope for unity. To the postmodern, there is no unity toward which to strive. All is fragments.

Through it all, however, runs this thread of Idealism, holding out a hope that we can unify the terrible schism in our nature. The work takes place in the mind; in fact, *is* the mind, which for Emerson is the field of battle. The so-called mind/body split is not, for him, the problem. It is the mind that lacks integrity, and as he said in "Self-

Reliance," "Nothing at last is sacred but the integrity of your own mind."

The sacred becomes synonymous with a mind at one with Universal Being. The mind becomes reunited, reinsphered, and reassured. We are *re*-minded, in effect, by the process of integration.

Finding the True Self

Surprise or lack of expectation is the key to the experience of unity or integration. We cannot will such revelation, nor can we control the mind by any manipulation of mental processes. Emerson was quite clear about the origin and quality of these experiences. Any philosophy which we might employ to help us recover our integrity of mind has to lead into this realm of unity without employing mechanical aids. Emerson's philosophy was based on a natural leading and was effective because his language—sentences, paragraphs, essays—did in *form* what they suggested in *meaning*.

For example, in the beginning of his essay "Experience" Emerson asks a question which addresses two aspects of our nature and, in effect, brings them together momentarily in a unity of consideration. His question reaches into that part of ourselves which searches for a ground of being and into that more mundane part which seeks out the foundation of our daily experience. His question is, "Where do we find ourselves?"

The more mundane half of the question asks, "Where [in the succession of life's experiences] do we find ourselves [at the moment]?" The other asks, "Where do we [look to] find our [true] selves?" The rest of the essay searches out an answer to both questions. In fact, all of Emerson's work seeks answers to these two aspects of the question.

We might jump ahead for a moment to see how the question has progressed since Emerson asked it in the 1840s. It surprises us in the light of his own overall philosophical stance that Friedrich Nietzsche was strongly influenced by Emerson, so much so that in the preface to *The Genealogy of Morals* (1887) he takes Emerson's question (whether consciously or not we don't know) and recasts it for a later time. "We have never searched for ourselves—how should it come to pass, that we should ever find ourselves?" Further on, he answers the question, prefiguring the radically divided self of the twentieth century:

> Of necessity we remain strangers to ourselves, we understand ourselves not, in ourselves we are bound to be mistaken, for of us holds good to all eternity the motto, "Each one is farthest away from himself"—as far as ourselves are concerned we are not "knowers."

Today, we are not only not "knowers" but find ourselves inundated by forces which deny even the attempt. We are flooded by the data of the culture, and we are unable to discriminate clearly among the alternatives that demand our attention. Our inability to step back, to detach ourselves from experience, to take stock or just to rest a moment to catch our philosophical breath, as it were, is palpable. Even the usual spiritual practices seem to fail to stem the tide, and by day's end we are so inundated by this data (mostly electronic) that we have become simply transmitters, sort of relay stations, receiving data and passing it along (for a price) to someone else. We become merely the mechanisms that serve the thirst for more information. Unfortunately, we serve only the static of survival and there is no possibility of addressing the second part of our question: Where do we look to find our true selves?

Our situation is dire. Emerson said in "Demonology" that if we could catch a glimpse of our true condition we would barely be restrained from suicide. He meant that "our true condition" was so far removed from the natural order of things that we might despair of ever recovering our true selves. In fact, Nietzsche's glimpse into this fundamental disparity drove him mad. Most human beings, however, are safe from self-destruction, for the most part, because rather than seeing truly, we prefer to sleep, to remain unconsciously part of the surface of things.

The Path to Self-Recovery

Therefore, given the extent of the need, what does Emerson offer in the way of helpful philosophy to relieve our anguish and perhaps help us to recover? As a true philosopher, he stays away from didactic solutions or systems, both of which limit our choices as well as the power of our self-perceptions. A passage in "Considerations by the Way" sets the tone of Emerson's philosophical approach:

> Although this garrulity of advising is born with us, I confess that life is rather a subject of wonder, than of didactics. So much fate, so much irresistible dictation from temperament and unknown inspiration enters into it, that we doubt that we can say anything out of our experience whereby to help each other.

Philosophy is not guidance. It is, as we noted above, "the

account which the human mind gives to itself of the constitution of the world." And since we are made of the
same stuff as the world is, our knowledge of the world
forms the basis of our knowledge of ourselves.

The capacity for wonder is essential because without
it we narrow our vision too quickly, expect too little of
our questioning. Emerson lists fate, temperament, and
inspiration as influences which overpower useful advice
in life. Fate is "the limitations of my inheritance and the
natural world." It is not, in Emerson's view, a matter of
predestination, except insofar as genetics predisposes us
to illness, talents, or span of life. Temperament may be
somewhat more in our control, but even here, we are too
much in the grasp of hormonal tendencies to claim any
freedom from them. Last, unknown inspiration is the
province of a hidden power and comes to us mysterious-
ly to lead our better actions and our creativity.

One answer to the question of how we find ourselves—in the philosophic sense of our true selves—is to
be found in setting out on the journey to self-recovery, to
what Emerson referred to again and again as the erect
position. We might say that it is a journey from the sleep-
ing to the wakened state, from the supine to the standing. If in life "eighty percent of success is just showing
up," then eighty percent of philosophy is waking up. The
other twenty is discipline.

In "Experience" we are reminded that the first step
in any serious attempt to know ourselves is awakening to
the possibility of entering the door to self-knowledge.

But the Genius which, according to the old belief,
stands at the door by which we enter, and gives us
the lethe to drink, that we may tell no tales, mixed
the cup too strongly, and we cannot shake off the

lethargy now at noonday. Sleep lingers all our lifetime about our eyes, as night hovers all day in the
boughs of the fir-tree. All things swim and glitter.
Our life is not so much threatened as our perception.

And perception is the point of departure. Certainly
we can recognize ourselves as being unable to "shake off
the lethargy now at noonday." And we can also recognize that the self-knowledge we seek is not merely a
matter of being more alert in the ordinary sense of that
word, like being "wired" or on a caffeine high. What
Emerson tells us is that we tend to shut down in the face
of daily life and remain satisfied with the surfaces of
things. Mechanical actions dominate our days, and just as
we are content to lose ourselves in the deceptions of a
good movie, so are we content to lose ourselves in life's
imagery. This false withdrawal represents a dangerous
development in human culture and the conduct of life.

The paragraph that concludes "Considerations by
the Way" lays out the essential points of practical self-
recovery:

> The secret of culture is to learn that a few great
> points steadily reappear, alike in the poverty of the
> obscurest farm, and in the miscellany of metropoli-
> tan life, and that these few are alone to be regard-
> ed,—the escape from all false ties; courage to be
> what we are; and love of what is simple and beauti-
> ful; independence, and cheerful relation, these are
> the essentials,—these, and the wish to serve,—to
> add somewhat to the well-being of men.

These great points are a summary statement, published
as part of *The Conduct of Life* in 1860, very near the end
of Emerson's publishing life.

Beyond the Games We Play

The escape from all false ties is a reference to our dependence on illusion. If we go back for a moment to Nietzsche's question ("—how should it come to pass, that we should ever find ourselves?"), the first place we need to look is in the elaborate construct of illusions we and the world have built for us.

Emerson defined illusions as the games and masks of our self-deception. At the most basic level of our existence, we react with fear to every apparent threat from our environment. Our lowest instinct—fight or flight—stimulates the creation of a stock of these games and masks in order to protect, deflect, justify, and escape from whatever appears to threaten us. Gradually, these deceptions sheath us in a protective armor to allow us to remain somewhere between the extremes of complete escape (flight) or inhuman violence (fight). The habit of illusion-building at this low level of experience grows to encompass higher levels of experience. By the time we are adults we have clothed ourselves in such elaborate illusions that the task of stripping them away becomes in itself an object of great fear.

Emerson's gift to us in his writing is the compassion with which he helps us strip away illusions. Compared to his friend and companion Henry David Thoreau, Emerson is saintly in his guidance. Thoreau, in *Walden* and *Civil Disobedience*, shows little patience for self-deception as he hammers away at our games and masks. This from Walden:

> Moral reform is the effort to throw off sleep. Why is it that men give so poor an account of their day if they have not been slumbering? They are not such poor calculators. If they had not been overcome

with drowsiness, they would have performed something. The millions are awake enough for physical
labor; but only one in a million is awake enough for
effective intellectual exertion, only one in a hundred
millions to a poetic or divine life. To be awake is to
be alive. I have never met a man who was quite
awake. How could I have looked him in the face?

We must learn to reawaken and keep ourselves
awake, not by mechanical aids, but by an infinite
expectation of the dawn, which does not forsake us
in our soundest sleep. I know of no more encouraging fact than the unquestionable ability of man to
elevate his life by a conscious endeavor.

Encouraging to be sure, but tough. The identification
of illusion with sleep was typical of both Thoreau and
Emerson. Drowsiness becomes a description of the unex-
amined life. To be awake was to be in a state of
detached self-observation, what Emerson called reflection
at the beginning of "Spiritual Laws."

When the act of reflection takes place in the
mind, when we look at ourselves in the light of
thought, we discover that our life is enbosomed in
beauty.

This observation reminds us that the act of reflection
"takes place in the mind." It is not intentional or directed
by the will. Reflection "takes place" in that part of the
mind which receives insight. It is a gift. Our intention is
to expect the gift, or to place ourselves in an attitude of
thoughtful expectation.

Modern philosophy has engaged itself thoroughly in
the investigation of the nature of thinking, particularly,

the nature of intuitive thought (as opposed to cursive or logical thinking). The work of Martin Heidegger addresses itself to this concern with frustratingly difficult, but nonetheless remarkable analysis.

Heidegger's *Discourse on Thinking* was the result of notes taken in 1944–45 from a conversation between a teacher, a scholar, and a scientist. Its subject is meditative thinking, which is very close to Emerson's concept of intuitive reflection. In the conversation between the three thinkers, Heidegger begins by suggesting that thinking and willing are not to be related and that, properly seen, human thinking begins in waiting for thought to arise and involves what he called *Gelassenheit*, an English approximation of which is "releasement." As the scholar says at one point, "So far as we can wean ourselves from willing, we contribute to the awakening of releasement." "Releasement" in such a noun form removes the causal from the action. In proper thinking, something called releasement simply happens or, "takes places."

The conversation proceeds to attempt to define a whole new set of terms:

> Scholar: To be sure I don't know yet what the word releasement means; but I seem to presage that releasement awakens when our nature is let-in so as to have dealings with that which is not a willing.
> Scientist: You speak without letup of a letting-be and give the impression that what is meant is a kind of passivity. All the same, I think I understand that it is in no way a matter of weakly allowing things to slide and drift along.
> Scholar: Perhaps a higher acting is concealed in

releasement than is found in all the actions within the world and in the machinations of all mankind . . .

Teacher: . . . which higher acting is yet no activity.

Scientist: Then releasement lies—if we may use the word lie—beyond the distinction between activity and passivity . . .

Scholar: . . . because releasement does *not* belong to the domain of the will.

Scientist: The transition from willing into releasement is what seems difficult to me.

Teacher: And all the more, since the nature of releasement is still hidden.

Scholar: Especially so because even releasement can still be thought of as within the domain of will, as is the case with old masters of thought such as Meister Eckhart.

Teacher: From whom, all the same, much can be learned.

Scholar: Certainly; but what we have called releasement evidently does not mean casting off sinful selfishness and letting self-will go in favor of the divine will.

Teacher: No, not that.

Scientist: In many respects it is clear to me what the word releasement should not signify for us. But at the same time, I know less and less what we are talking about. . . .

(*Discourse on Thinking*, [New York: Harper Torchbooks, 1966], 60, 61–62)

We share the difficulty of the scientist, who is gradually letting go of all his preconceived formulations. The teacher is almost already through the most difficult part of the process and is therefore able to connect thoughts to the common theme. The domain they all seek is a special region that approaches the transcendent horizon, where human thought, when it arises, finds a harmony with universal law. In "Spiritual Laws," Emerson called this intersection a place where "the infinite lies stretched in smiling repose." It is the image of the reclining Buddha.

Emerson is unique in American philosophy because at an early stage in his development he incorporated Eastern philosophy into his Idealism. His study of Hindu texts, even as early as his Boston Latin days, kept the vision of Unity strong and gave him an articulation of illusion not available in Western texts. In one of his notebooks, entitled "Orientalist," Emerson reflects on the idea of illusion from the perspective of the Vedas.

> In the history of intellect no more important fact than the Hindoo [sic] theology, teaching that the beatitudes or Supreme Good is to be obtained through science; namely, by perception of the real and unreal, setting aside matter, and qualities and affections, or emotions and persons and actions as *Maias* or illusions, and thus arriving at the contemplation of the One Eternal Life and Cause and a perpetual approach and assimilation to Him; thus escaping new births and transmigration.
>
> The highest object of their religion was to restore that bond by which their own self (*atman*) was linked to the Eternal Self (*paramatman*); to recover that unity which had been clouded and obscured by the magical illusions of reality, by the so-called *Maia* of Creation.

All false ties are the illusions which keep us from recovering that essential unity, and the first step in peeling them away is to know that they are there. Like all exercises in self-study, there are ways of knowing what is real work and what is self-indulgence. Exchanging one illusion for another solves nothing, and the ego can be very clever in playing games of substitution.

It seems an impertinence to suggest that most of what takes place in our minds all day is none of our business. Once an individual awakens to thought amid the chaos of daily existence, the usual sorts of inner conversations, self-justifications, and fantasies have no place in our perceptions. Reflective thought is a discipline like meditation and has to be watched. Emerson commented once that we were fortunate if when dreaming through the woods we were wakened to thought by the scream of an eagle. The eagle is an image of our higher capacities of perception, and it is grace when that organ of thought calls us to attention. So challenging is this process that Emerson's articulation of it requires a different vocabulary, including words like "strict" and "severe." In "Illusions" we are given some guidance.

> In this kingdom of illusions we grope eagerly for stays and foundations. There is none but a strict and faithful dealing at home, and a severe barring out of all duplicity or illusion there. Whatever games are played with us, we must play no games with our selves, but deal in our privacy with the last honesty and truth.

Indeed, the character of Emerson's "strict and faithful dealing at home" was an anarchic freedom, so radical when he proposed it that few critics of his views appreciated its implications. As civilization has "progressed," so to speak, so has the radical necessity to be free from its deadening influence. Integrity of mind is a radical free-

dom because to achieve it means being "an endless seeker with no Past at my back," as he said in "Circles." It is a
tall order: no tradition, no influence, no system, no
teachers. As he said in a late journal entry (1866), ". . .
for every seeing soul there are two absorbing facts,—I
and the Abyss." The Abyss in this reference is not an
existential Nothingness, but rather the freedom from the
Past so essential to the erect position. To see the Abyss
as Nothingness is just another illusion. Perceived honestly, the Abyss has to be the Unknown, or, if we must have
an image, the "undiscover'd country from whose bourn/
No traveler returns," as Hamlet says.

What Emerson accomplished in his own self-recovery, over a lifetime of endless seeking, was a record of
thought we continue to characterize as practical idealism
because, radical though it was, it still celebrates the
infinitude of human possibility in the face of the Great
Unknown within a perceived order which is inherently
sublime.

> And so I think that the last lesson of life, the
> choral song which rises from all elements and all
> angels, is, a voluntary obedience, a necessitated
> freedom. Man is made of the same atoms as the
> world is, he shares the same impressions, predispo-
> sitions, and destiny. When his mind is illuminated,
> when his heart is kind, he throws himself joyfully
> into the sublime order, and does, with knowledge,
> what the stones do by structure. ("Worship")

An Emerson Chronology

1803   May 25. Born in Boston, Mass., second oldest of eight children.

1811   Father, William Emerson, dies, leaving family without adequate support.

1812–17 Attends Boston Latin School.

1817   Enrolls at Harvard College, age 14; works as orderly to president; waits on tables.

1819   Begins to keep a journal.

1821   Graduates with A.B. degree, 30th in class of 59.

1821–25 Teaches school, mostly in brother William's school for young women.

1825–27 Attends Divinity College at Harvard.

1828   ʼEngagement to Ellen Tucker announced.

1829   Marries; named Junior Pastor at Second Church, Boston.

1831   Wife, Ellen, dies of tuberculosis.

1832   Resigns post at Second Church; sails for Europe on Dec. 25.

1833   Visits Malta, Italy, France, England, and Scotland; meets Coleridge, Wordsworth, Carlyle.

1834   Returns to America; settles in Concord, Mass.

1835   Marries Lydia Jackson.

1836   Son Waldo born; publishes *Nature* anonymously.

1837   Delivers Phi Beta Kappa address at Harvard, entitled "The American Scholar."

1838   Delivers "An Address" at Divinity College; strongly attacked by religious establishment. Does not return to Harvard for thirty years.

1839   Daughter Ellen born.

1841   Publishes *Essays: First Series*; daughter Edith born.

1842   Son Waldo dies, age five years, of scarlet fever.

1844   Publishes *Essays: Second Series*; son Edward born.

1847–48 Lectures throughout England and Scotland.

1850   Publishes *Representative Men*.

1856   Publishes *English Traits*.

1860   Publishes *The Conduct of Life*.

1872   Fire in upper story of Concord house; travels to Europe and Egypt with daughter Ellen while repairs are made. Stops lecturing and writing.

1882   April 27, dies at home in Concord; buried in Sleepy Hollow Cemetery.

PART TWO
Selections from Emerson's Writings

The Introduction
to *Nature*

The essential texts of Ralph Waldo Emerson include the following: *Nature; Essays: First Series; Essays: Second Series; Representative Men; The Conduct of Life; English Traits*; and three lectures published independently as essays: "The Transcendentalist," "The American Scholar," and "An Address," delivered at the Divinity College at Harvard. Of lesser importance are later collected essays entitled *Society and Solitude* and *Letters and Social Aims*. The collected poems are certainly important but are secondary. Relevant to an understanding of his vision, however, are the following poems: "The Problem," "Uriel," "Hamatreya," "Threnody," "Brahma," and "Terminus." Serious students of Emerson will study his journals, particularly those written between 1835 and 1844.

The choice of texts for this book was based on two factors: first, a sample of those essays which reveal most directly the philosophy behind the work; and second, the demands of space. The five essays included are not printed in chronological order of composition. They represent an introduction to sources, vocabulary, development of thought, and mature vision. Each selection has a brief, separate introduction.

As an introduction to these texts, I have chosen to

deal in some detail with the introduction to *Nature*, Emerson's first published work. Although this small book was published anonymously in 1836 (as was the custom for such manifestos), it was quickly recognized as Emerson's and soon acquired a small but ardent following. Emerson was thirty-three when he published *Nature* and had recently returned from Europe, where he had traveled after the death of his first wife and after his resignation from his post as a minister. In England, he had met Coleridge, Wordsworth and Carlyle, all of whom had been influential in his early thinking. Only Carlyle lived up to his expectations, however, and the two became life-long correspondents.

Nature was begun as Emerson made the long sea journey to America and was completed after he had settled in Concord and commenced his new career as a lecturer. What follows is the introduction to the text.

> A subtle chain of countless rings
> The next unto the farthest brings;
> The eye reads omens where it goes,
> And speaks all languages the rose;
> And, striving to be man, the worm
> Mounts through all the spires of form.

Our age is retrospective. It builds the sepulchres of the fathers. It writes biographies, histories, and criticism. The foregoing generations beheld God and nature face to face; we, through their eyes. Why should not we also enjoy an original relation to the universe? Why should not we have a poetry and philosophy of insight and not of tradition, and a religion by revelation to us, and not the history of theirs? Embosomed for a season in nature, whose floods of life stream around and through us, and

invite us by the powers they supply, to action proportioned to nature, why should we grope among
the dry bones of the past, or put the living generation into masquerade out of its faded wardrobe? The
sun shines to-day also. There is more wool and flax
in the fields. There are new lands, new men, new
thoughts. Let us demand our own works and laws
and worship.

Undoubtedly we have no questions to ask
which are unanswerable. We must trust the perfection of the creation so far, as to believe that whatever curiosity the order of things has awakened in our
minds, the order of things can satisfy. Every man's
condition is a solution in hieroglyphic to those
inquiries he would put. He acts it as life, before he
apprehends it as truth. In like manner, nature is
already, in its forms and tendencies, describing its
own design. Let us interrogate the great apparition,
that shines so peacefully around us. Let us inquire,
to what end is nature?

All science has one aim, namely, to find a theory of nature. We have theories of races and of functions, but scarcely yet a remote approach to an idea
of creation. We are now so far from the road to
truth, that religious teachers dispute and hate each
other, and speculative men are esteemed unsound
and frivolous. But to a sound judgment, the most
abstract truth is the most practical. Whenever a true
theory appears, it will be its own evidence. Its test
is, that it will explain all phenomena. Now many are
thought not only unexplained but inexplicable; as
language, sleep, madness, dreams, beasts, sex.

Philosophically considered, the universe is com-
posed of Nature and the Soul. Strictly speaking,

therefore, all that is separate from us, all which Philosophy distinguishes as the NOT ME, that is, both nature and art, all other men and my own body, must be ranked under this name, NATURE. In enumerating the values of nature and casting up their sum, I shall use the word in both senses;— in its common and in its philosophical import. In inquiries so general as our present one, the inaccuracy is not material; no confusion of thought will occur. *Nature*, in the common sense, refers to essences unchanged by man; space, the air, the river, the leaf. *Art* is applied to the mixture of his will with the same things, as in a house, a canal, a statue, a picture. But his operations taken together are so insignificant, a little chipping, baking, patching, and washing, that in an impression so grand as that of the world on the human mind, they do not vary the result.

*   *   *

In this introduction, a little more than five hundred words in length, Emerson inscribed the first small circle of his philosophy. In the remainder of his work, embodying a lifetime of reflection, he expanded "a subtle chain of countless rings" to encompass the full range of human nature and experience. Like Homer and Shakespeare before him, he carved with his pen a vision of the human condition—body, mind, spirit—in strict relation to nature, and in the process answered the questions posed in his first small circle of thought.

Our age is retrospective. It builds the sepulchres of the fathers. It writes biographies, histories, and criticism.

The first problem Emerson addresses is lack of immediacy, dependence on the past, leaving us burdened with second-hand knowledge, separated from our own nature and from any relation to the creation. Although we still write biographies, histories, and criticism, we do not write much philosophy. Even philosophers seldom write philosophy any more. The so-called mainstream of the profession confines itself to dealing with the nature of language and arguments about what we may say and not say. We have become so paralyzed by such investigation and the resulting cacophony of opinion that we have become alienated from ourselves and from nature, to the extent that we find ourselves in a post-modern culture devoid of life-enhancing articulation and direction. Our philosophy appears on tee-shirts which read "Nothing is true; everything is possible." In a journal entry dated 19 April, 1836, Emerson said, "The philosopher should explain to us the laws of redeeming the time" (JMN, V, 149).

> The foregoing generations beheld God and nature face to face; we, through their eyes. Why should not we also enjoy an original relation to the universe? Why should not we have a poetry and philosophy of insight and not of tradition, and a religion by revelation to us, and not the history of theirs?

Here is the crux. Emerson's two questions can also be read declaratively as a ground for philosophical being, as in: We must have an original relation to the universe, a poetry and a philosophy of insight, and a religion of direct revelation to us. This ground forms the basis of Emerson's Idealism. It does not deny the past, which should always serve as a measure of the truth against which our immediate insights are tested. It does, how-

ever, put the past in its place and relieve us of the need
to constantly revise it into some measure of relevancy. In
other words, we do not have to think of a Gothic cathe-
dral or the works of Aquinas as standards of spiritual
expression from which we have, alas, fallen away.
Instead, they can be seen for what they are: accurate
expressions of medieval spiritual sensibility and genius.
Here in this time and place, we have our own questions
and our own means of inquiry and expression. We need
our own insights and our own philosophy. The principle
is quite simple: If we do not recognize the ground on
which we find ourselves standing as the authentic setting
for inquiry, we are forced to deny our existence and to
search longingly for what is past and therefore second-
hand or to look wistfully into a future we cannot ever
hope to influence. Both wisdom and practicality demand
that we give our strict attention to the ground which we
occupy and, doing so, read attentively the messages it
sends.

Implicit in this immediate ground is a constant need
for freedom and transformation. Emerson's call to freedom is not a call to anarchy. The task of inquiry, the
demands of insight, and the rigors of revelation are
immense, much more difficult to master than the comfortable dependence on the past. As a result, most people find it easier to accept ancient doctrines than to
develop the intuitive powers of reflection and observation leading to authentic insights. And as we see so clearly in cults and extremes of religious thought, dogmatism
and fanaticism take away freedom and replace it with
blinding obedience and devotion. Emerson reflected on
the risk of this freedom from tradition in "Self-Reliance"
when he wrote,

THE INTRODUCTION TO *NATURE*

I remember an answer which when quite young I was prompted to make to a valued adviser, who was wont to importune me with the dear old doctrines of the church. On my saying, "What have I to do with the sacredness of traditions, if I live wholly from within?" my friend suggested, But these impulses may be from below, not from above." I replied, "They do not seem to me to be such; but if I am the Devil's child, I will live then from the Devil." No law can be sacred to me but that of my nature.

This self-trust marks the beginning of wisdom and the first step on the royal road to self-knowledge. Those who see themselves as the arbiters of sacred tradition and revelation will always call Emerson's declaration dangerous and arrogant. Philosophically, however, such independence and self-reliance are both necessary and proper.

Here, as in all of his work, Emerson relieves the tension created by assertions of independence with qualifications. In—" this instance he sets forth this principle: "No law can be sacred to me but that of my nature." The next question, then, has to be, "What is our nature?"

Emerson answers that question in the rest of *Nature* and in the collections of essays and lectures which followed it, and the reader is urged to read *Nature* in addition to the essays selected for this brief sample of Emerson's work. The inquiry in *Nature* proceeds:

Undoubtedly we have no questions to ask which are unanswerable. We must trust the perfection of the creation so far, as to believe that whatever curiosity the order of things has awakened in our minds, the order of things can satisfy.

How different is this assertion of confidence in the power of the human mind from the traditional view which placed limits on human knowledge in a universe seen as far from perfect. The universe is perfect insofar as it obeys unerringly a few fundamental laws, principles which rule every aspect of existence from the movement of galaxies to the motions within atoms. The chaos we experience in the world, even the randomness perceived at the subatomic level, is illusory. As Emerson said in "Compensation," "The dice of God are always loaded." Suspended somewhere between the extremes of galactic motion and seeming chaos, human experience is subject to these same universal laws, and having knowledge of these laws is as much our destiny as our nature.

> Every man's condition is a solution in hieroglyphic to those inquiries he would put. He acts it as life, before he apprehends it as truth.

Here is a statement that folds in on itself and is a definition of self-inquiry in relation to human experience. The reference to hieroglyphics arose for Emerson amid the tremendous interest generated early in his century by the deciphering of the Rosetta Stone, which turned out to be the key to temple hieroglyphics in Egypt. Emerson saw that each person's experience was a symbolic answer to the spiritual questions which naturally formed in the mind. Proper attention given to personal experience unlocked the door to self-knowledge. An examination of another's experience was nothing but gossip, or at best, opinion. The discipline of self-examination, or reflection, reveals circle upon circle of perception and affects a revolution in how we perceive our nature. In this instance Emers on follows the ancient doctrine "Know Thyself" as the point of departure.

> Whenever a true theory appears, it will be its own
> evidence. Its test is that it will explain all phenomena.

What Emerson hints at here is what the twentieth century
calls the Unified Field. Still to be articulated, at least in
finite mathematical terms, it has nonetheless been
expressed for thousands of years in the Hindu Vedas and
in the enigmatic sentences of pre-Socratic thinkers from
Thales to Heraclitus. What fascinates is Emerson's statement, "it will be its own evidence." How are we to think
of that? Just before this he said, "But to a sound judgment, the most abstract truth is the most practical." What
is practical is useful in daily life, in answering the problems of existence. What is abstract is formed in our consciousness as an idea, something which takes shape from
the laws which form the basis of existence itself.
Therefore, if there is to be a relationship between an idea
of existence and the actual experience of it, it were best
if the theory and the experience be identical or fused
into a unity. All is One, said the ancients, and they saw
that as consistent with their philosophical experience.

In this unity, however, are aspects, divisions of reality.

> Philosophically considered, the universe is com-
> posed of Nature and the Soul. Strictly speaking,
> therefore, all that is separate from us, all which
> Philosophy distinguishes as the NOT ME, that is,
> both nature and art, all other men and my own
> body, must be ranked under this name, NATURE.

Emerson's NOT ME is the manifest world and includes
his (and our) own body. In referring to his own body as
"the office where I work," he was making a crucial distinction between the I that worked and the instrument
that served the needs of this "I." Soul, for Emerson, is

connected to Mind or consciousness, which in turn exists in a hierarchy of refinement, from the purity of the Universal Mind to the limited consciousness of the animal kingdom, Human beings are in a middle position, thinking their own egotistical thoughts or, in moments of great clarity, penetrating the veil to the consciousness of the Over-Soul.

The beauty of these distinctions in Emerson's vision is that nature is not fundamentally "other"; rather, this NOT ME is caused by and is a manifestation of consciousness and gives us daily, hourly, even moment-by-moment signs to be read by the attentive eye and ear. And, so, if we are alert and if our perceptions are accurate, the fundamental unity of the universal construct reveals itself to us, and in the presence of such revelation we are lifted out of the ordinary into the extra-ordinary, or transcendent.

The Essay
"Plato, or the
Philosopher"

This ordered universe (*cosmos*) which is the same for all, was not created by any one of the gods or of mankind, but it was ever and is and shall be ever-living Fire, kindled in measure and quenched in measure. HERACLITUS

In "Plato, or the Philosopher," Emerson affirms the means by which all great thinkers function: absorption and synthesis. Plato absorbed the work of the pre-Socratics, including Heraclitus, and then, because he was capable of greater synthesis and thirsted for more, traveled to Italy and Egypt and, probably, into India to absorb and synthesize even more. In his own right, Emerson, too, absorbed what he called the "lustres" of his predecessors, including Heraclitus, and it was this quality that he admired so in Plato.

In "Uses of Great Men," the introduction to his third volume of essays, *Representative Men*, published in 1850, Emerson spelled out his vision of genius and its relation to nature. There are echoes of Heraclitus in the following passage:

The possibility of interpretation lies in the identity of
the observer with the observed. Each material thing
has its celestial side; has its translation, through
humanity, into the spiritual and necessary sphere,
where it plays a part as indestructible as any other.
And to these, their ends, all things continually
ascend. The gases gather to the solid firmament: the
chemic lump arrives at the plant, and grows; arrives
at the quadruped, and walks; arrives at the man, and
thinks. But also the constituency determines the vote
of the representative. He is not only representative,
but participant. Like can only be known by like. The
reason why he knows about them is, that he is of
them: he has just come out of nature, or from being
a part of that thing.

In *Nature*, where we read that the "worm mounts
through all the spires of form," Emerson began his
description of the progress of the soul in matter. In "The
American Scholar" he described Man Thinking as the
archetypal human being properly aligned to the laws of
nature. In "Representative Men" he adds to the great circle of his vision by describing the cosmic force, or
Heraclitian Fire, in various representative figures whose
genius in turn inscribes the whole of human expression.
His selection, worked out painstakingly from 1844 in an
initial lecture on Napoleon, until the publication of the
completed text in 1850, includes six representative figures: Plato, the philosopher; Swedenborg, the mystic;
Montaigne, the skeptic; Shakespeare, the poet; Napoleon,
the man of action; and Goethe, the writer. They are all
Emerson.

The decision to move away from the archetypal Man
Thinking seen in "The American Scholar" was not a

change in his thinking, some fracturing of his vision, but a natural progression. His representative figures are still aspects of the whole and are held up not so much as (to use a contemporary image) "role models," as to illustrate the way human beings embody the forces of creation differently to the proper ends of creative expression. We are not to emulate Plato or Shakespeare, but rather to see in their expression the diverse possibilities for our own.

Even though his friend Henry Thoreau could wonder why he had not included Jesus in his pantheon of genius, it is clear that Emerson intended to focus his attention on attributes and not on personalities. He could have written an essay entitled "Jesus Christ, or the Prophet," but in so doing would have had to expose to scrutiny his view that Jesus was of the race of men and was not God. He had already been the subject of much criticism for declaring in his "Divinity School Address" that Jesus, ". . . alone in all history . . . estimated the greatness of man." It would not in 1850 have served a useful purpose to engage in a destructive debate with the opinions and dogmas of established religious thinking.

It was just this sort of opinionated reaction that Emerson meant to silence in beginning his text with Plato. As he said in "Uses of Great Men," "Without Plato, we should almost lose our faith in the possibility of a reasonable book." This remark came at the end of a passage concerning the foibles of human opinion-holding. Plato's great contribution to human thought was the clarity and thoroughness with which he delineated the truth from opinions (*doxa* in the Greek). The examined life was meant to provide us with the means, called discrimination, of examining our opinions, those rigid ideas we hold that seem to define us and give us our reasons to exist. Nothing is more destructive than the self-righteousness we exhibit in our competitive, opinion-holding relation to others. As Emerson commented, "I go to a convention of philanthropists. Do what I can, I cannot keep my eyes off the clock" ("Uses of Great Men"). It is philosophy that provides the opportunity to rise above these complacencies into another realm. Plato was that "balanced soul" who drove relentlessly to the truth and left the *doxa* of human interaction scattered like ashes in the wind.

PLATO, or The Philosopher

Among secular books, Plato only is entitled to Omar's fanatical compliment to the Koran, when he said, "Burn the libraries; for their value is in this book." These sentences contain the culture of nations; these are the corner-stone of schools; these are the fountain-head of literatures. A discipline it is in logic, arithmetic, taste, symmetry, poetry, language, rhetoric, ontology, morals, or practical wisdom. There was never such range of speculation. Out of Plato come all things that are still written and debated among men of thought. Great havoc makes he among our originalities. We have reached the mountain from which all these drift boulders were detached. The Bible of the learned for twenty-two hundred years, every brisk young man, who says in succession fine things to each reluctant generation,—Boethius, Rabelais, Erasmus, Bruno, Locke, Rousseau, Alfieri, Coleridge,—is some reader of Plato, translating into the vernacular, wittily, his good things. Even the men of grander proportion suffer some deduction from the misfortune (shall I say?) of coming after this exhausting generalizer. St. Augustine, Copernicus, Newton, Behmen,

Swedenborg, Goethe, are likewise his debtors and must say after him. For it is fair to credit the broadest generalizer with all the particulars deducible from his thesis.

Plato is philosophy, and philosophy, Plato,—at once the glory and the shame of mankind, since neither Saxon nor Roman have availed to add any idea to his categories. No wife, no children had he, and the thinkers of all civilized nations are his posterity and are tinged with his mind. How many great men Nature is incessantly sending up out of night, to be his men,—Platonists! the Alexandrians, a constellation of genius; the Elizabethans, not less; Sir Thomas More, Henry More, John Hales, John Smith, Lord Bacon, Jeremy Taylor, Ralph Cudworth, Sydenham, Thomas Taylor; Marcilius Ficinus, and Picus Mirandola. Calvinism is in his Phaedo: Christianity is in it. Mahometanism draws all its philosophy, in its handbook of morals, the Akhlak-y-Jalaly, from him. Mysticism finds in Plato all its texts. This citizen of a town in Greece is no villager nor patriot. An Englishman reads and says, 'how English!' a German,—'how Teutonic!' an Italian,—'how Roman and how Greek!' As they say that Helen of Argos, had that universal beauty that every body felt related to her, so Plato seems, to a reader in New England, an American genius. His broad humanity transcends all sectional lines.

This range of Plato instructs us what to think of the vexed question concerning his reputed works,—what are genuine, what spurious. It is singular that wherever we find a man higher, by a whole head, than any of his contemporaries, it is sure to come into doubt what are his real works. Thus Homer, Plato, Raffaelle, Shakspeare. For these men magnetise their contemporaries, so that their companions can do for them what they can never do for themselves; and the great man does thus live in several bodies, and write, or paint, or act, by many hands; and, after some time, it is not easy to say what is the authentic work of the master, and what is only of his school.

Plato, too, like every great man, consumed his own times. What is a great man, but one of great affinities, who takes up into himself all arts, sciences, all knowables, as his food? He can spare nothing; he can dispose of every thing. What is not good for virtue, is good for knowledge. Hence his contemporaries tax him with plagiarism. But the inventor only knows how to borrow; and society is glad to forget the innumerable laborers who ministered to this architect, and reserves all its gratitude for him. When we are praising Plato, it seems we are praising quotations from Solon, and Sophron, and Philolaus. Be it so. Every book is a quotation; and every house is a quotation out of all forests, and mines, and stone quarries; and every man is a quotation from all his ancestors. And this grasping inventor puts all nations under contribution.

Plato absorbed the learning of his times,—Philolaus, Timaeus, Heraclitus, Parmenides, and what else; then his master, Socrates; and finding himself still capable of a larger synthesis,—beyond all example then or since,—he traveled into Italy, to gain what Pythagoras had for him; then into Egypt, and perhaps still farther east, to import the other element, which Europe wanted, into the European mind. This breadth entitles him to stand as the representative of philosophy. He says, in the Republic, "Such a genius as philosophers must of necessity have, is wont but seldom, in all its parts, to meet in one man; but its different parts generally spring up in different persons." Every man who would do any thing well, must come to it from a higher ground. A philosopher must be more than a philosopher. Plato is clothed with the powers of a poet, stands upon the highest place of the poet, and (though I doubt he wanted the decisive gift of lyric expression,) mainly is not a poet, because he chose to use the poetic gift to an ulterior purpose.

Great geniuses have the shortest biographies. Their cousins can tell you nothing about them. They lived in their writings, and so their house and street life was trivial and commonplace. If you would know their tastes and complexions, the most admiring of their readers most resembles them. Plato, especially, has no external biography. If he had lover, wife, or children, we hear nothing of them. He ground them all into paint. As a good chimney burns its smoke, so a philosopher converts the value of all his fortunes into his intellectual performances.

He was born 427, A.C. [B.C.E.], about the time of the death of Pericles; was of patrician connection in his times and city; and is said to have had an early inclination for war; but, in his twentieth year, meeting with Socrates, was easily dissuaded from this pursuit, and remained for ten years his scholar, until the death of Socrates. He then went to Megara; accepted the invitations of Dion and of Dionysius, to the court of Sicily; and went thither three times, though very capriciously treated. He traveled into Italy; then into Egypt, where he stayed a long time; some say three,—some say thirteen years. It is said he went farther, into Babylonia: this is uncertain. Returning to Athens, he gave lessons, in the Academy, to those whom his fame drew thither; and died, as we have received it, in the act of writing, at eighty-one years.

But the biography of Plato is interior. We are to account for the supreme elevation of this man, in the intellectual history of our race,—how it happens that in proportion to the culture of men, they become his scholars; that, as our Jewish Bible has implanted it self in the table-talk and household life of every man and woman in the European and American nations, so the writings of Plato have preoccupied every school of learning, every lover of thought, every church, every poet,—making it impossible to think, on certain levels, except through him. He stands between the truth and every man's mind, and has almost impressed language and the primary forms of thought, with his name and seal. I am struck, in reading him, with the extreme modernness of his style and spirit. Here is the germ of that Europe we know so well, in its long history of arts and arms: here are all its traits, already discernible in the mind of Plato,—and in none before him. It has spread itself since into a hundred histories, but has added no new element. This perpetual modernness is the measure of merit, in every work of art; since the author of it was not misled by any thing short-lived or local, but abode by real and abiding traits. How Plato came thus to be Europe, and philosophy, and almost literature, is the problem for us to solve.

This could not have happened, without a sound, sincere, and catholic man, able to honor, at the same time, the ideal, or laws of the mind, and fate, or the order of nature. The first period of a nation, as of an individual, is the period of unconscious strength. Children cry, scream, and stamp with fury, unable to express their desires. As soon as they can speak and tell their want, and the reason of it, they become gentle. In adult life, whilst the perceptions are obtuse, men and women talk vehemently and superlatively, blunder and quarrel: their manners are full of desperation; their speech is full of oaths. As soon as, with culture, things have cleared up a little, and they see them no longer in lumps and masses, but accurately distributed, they desist from that weak vehemence, and explain their meaning in detail. If the tongue had not been framed for articulation, man would still be a beast in the forest. The same weakness and want, on a higher plane, occurs daily in the education of ardent young men and women. 'Ah! you don't understand me; I have never met with any one who comprehends me': and they sigh and weep, write verses, and walk alone,—fault of power to express their precise meaning. In a month or two, through the favor of their good genius, they meet some one so related as to assist their volcanic estate; and, good communication being once established, they are thenceforward good citizens. It is ever thus. The progress is to accuracy, to skill, to truth, from blind force.

There is a moment in the history of every nation, when, proceeding out of this brute youth, the perceptive powers reach their ripeness, and have not yet become microscopic: so that man, at that instant, extends across the entire scale; and, with his feet still planted on the immense forces of night, converses, by his eyes and brain, with solar and stellar creation. That is the moment of adult health, the culmination of power.

Such is the history of Europe, in all points; and such in philosophy. Its early records, almost perished, are of the immigrations from Asia, bringing with them the dreams of barbarians; a confusion of crude notions of morals, and of natural philosophy, gradually subsiding through the partial insight of single teachers.

Before Pericles, came the Seven Wise Masters; and we have the beginnings of geometry, metaphysics, and ethics: then the partialists, —deducing the origin of things from flux or water, or from air, or from fire, or from mind. All mix with these causes mythologic pictures. At last, comes Plato, the distributor, who needs no barbaric paint, or tattoo, or whooping; for he can define. He leaves with Asia the vast and superlative; he is the arrival of accuracy and intelligence. "He shall be as a god to me, who can rightly divide and define."

This defining is philosophy. Philosophy is the account which the human mind gives to itself of the constitution of the world. Two cardinal facts lie forever at the base; the one, and the two. —1. Unity, or Identity; and, 2. Variety. We unite all things by perceiving the law which pervades them; by perceiving the superficial differences, and the profound resemblances. But every mental act,—this very perception of identity or oneness, recognizes the difference of things. Oneness and otherness. It is impossible to speak, or to think, without embracing both.

The mind is urged to ask for one cause of many effects; then for the cause of that; and again the cause, diving still into the profound: self-assured that it shall arrive at an absolute and sufficient one,—a one that shall be all. "In the midst of the sun is the light, in the midst of the light is truth, and in the midst of truth is the imperishable being," say the Vedas. All philosophy, of east and west, has the same centripetence. Urged by an opposite necessity, the mind returns from the one, to that which is not one, but other or many; from cause to effect; and affirms the necessary existence of variety, the self-existence of both, as each is involved in the other. These strictly-blended elements it is the problem of thought to separate, and to reconcile. Their existence is mutually contradictory and exclusive; and each so fast slides into the other, that we can never say what is one, and what it is not. The Proteus is as nimble in the highest as in the lowest grounds; when we contemplate the one, the true, the good,—as in the surfaces and extremities of matter.

In all nations, there are minds which incline to dwell in the conception of the fundamental Unity. The raptures of prayer and ecstasy of devotion lose all being in one Being. This tendency finds its highest expression in the religious writings of the East, and chiefly, in the Indian Scriptures, in the Vedas, the Bhagavat Geeta, and the Vishnu Purana. Those writings contain little else than this idea, and they rise to pure and sublime strains in celebrating it. The Same, the Same: friend and foe are of one stuff; the ploughman, the plough, and the furrow, are of one stuff; and the stuff is such, and so much, that the variations of form are unimportant. "You are fit," (says the supreme Krishna to a sage,) "to apprehend that you are not distinct from me. That which I am, thou art, and that also is this world, with its gods, and heroes, and mankind. Men contemplate distinctions, because they are stupefied with ignorance." "The words *I* and *mine* constitute ignorance. What is the great end of all, you shall now learn from me. It is soul,—one in all bodies, pervading, uniform, perfect, preeminent over nature, exempt from birth, growth, and decay, omnipresent, made up of true knowledge, independent, unconnected with unrealities, with name, species and the rest, in time past, present, and to come. The knowledge that this spirit, which is essentially one, is in one's own, and in all other bodies, is the wisdom of one who knows the unity of things. As one diffusive air, passing through the perforations of a flute, is distinguished as the notes of a scale, so the nature of the Great Spirit is single, though its forms be manifold, arising from the consequences of acts. When the difference of the investing form, as that of god, or the rest, is destroyed, there is no distinction." "The whole world is but a manifestation of Vishnu, who is identical with all things, and is to be regarded by the wise as not differing from, but as the same as themselves. I neither am going nor coming; nor is my dwelling in any one place; nor art thou, thou; nor are others, others; nor am I, I." As if he had said, 'All is for the soul, and the soul is Vishnu; and animals and stars are transient paintings; and light is whitewash; and durations are deceptive; and form is imprisonment; and heaven itself a decoy.' That which the soul seeks is resolution into being, above form, out of Tartarus, and out of heaven,—liberation from nature.

If speculation tends thus to a terrific unity, in which all things are absorbed, action tends directly backwards to diversity. The first is the course or gravitation of mind; the second is the power of nature. Nature is the manifold. The unity absorbs, and melts or reduces. Nature opens and creates. These two principles reappear and interpenetrate all things, all thought; the one, the many. One is being; the other, intellect: one is necessity; the other, freedom: one, rest; the other, motion: one, power; the other, distribution: one, strength; the other, pleasure: one, consciousness; the other, definition: one, genius; the other, talent: one, earnestness; the other, knowledge: one, possession; the other, trade: one, caste; the other, culture: one, king; the other, democracy: and, if we dare carry these generalizations a step higher, and name the last tendency of both, we might say, that the end of the one is escape from organization,—pure science; and the end of the other is the highest instrumentality, or use of means, or executive deity.

Each student adheres, by temperament and by habit, to the first or to the second of these gods of the mind. By religion, he tends to unity; by intellect, or by the senses, to the many. A too rapid unification, and an excessive appliance to parts and particulars, are the twin dangers of speculation.

To this partiality the history of nations corresponded. The country of unity, of immovable institutions, the seat of a philosophy delighting in abstractions, of men faithful in doctrine and in practice to the idea of a deaf, unimplorable, immense fate, is Asia; and it realizes this faith in the social institution of caste. On the other side, the genius of Europe is active and creative: it resists caste by culture; its philosophy was a discipline; it is a land of arts, inventions, trade, freedom. If the East loved infinity, the West delighted in boundaries.

European civility is the triumph of talent, the extension of system, the sharpened understanding, adaptive skill, delight in forms, delight in manifestation, in comprehensible results. Pericles, Athens, Greece, had been working in this element with the joy of genius not yet chilled by any foresight of the detriment of an excess. They saw before them no sinister political economy; no ominous Malthus; no Paris or London; no pitiless subdivision of classes,—the doom of the pin-makers, the doom of the weavers, of dressers, of stockingers, of carders, of spinners, of colliers; no Ireland; no Indian caste, superinduced by the efforts of Europe to throw it off. The understanding was in its health and prime. Art was in its splendid novelty. They cut the Pentelican marble as if it were snow, and their perfect works in architecture and sculpture seemed things of course, not more difficult than the completion of a new ship at the Medford yards, or new mills at Lowell. These things are in course, and may be taken for granted. The Roman legion, Byzantine legislation, English trade, the saloons of Versailles, the cafes of Paris, the steam-mill, steamboat, steam-coach, may all be seen in perspective; the town-meeting, the ballot-box, the news-paper and cheap press. Meantime, Plato, in Egypt and in eastern pilgrimages, imbibed the

idea of one Deity, in which all things are absorbed. The
unity of Asia and the detail of Europe; the infinitude of
the Asiatic soul, and the defining, result-loving, machine-
making, surface-seeking, opera-going Europe,—Plato
came to join, and, by contact, to enhance the energy of
each. The excellence of Europe and Asia are in his brain.
Metaphysics and natural philosophy expressed the
genius of Europe; he substructs the religion of Asia, as
the base.

In short, a balanced soul was born, perceptive of the
two elements. It is as easy to be great as to be small. The
reason why we do not at once believe in admirable souls,
is because they are not in our experience. In actual life,
they are so rare, as to be incredible; but, primarily, there
is not only no presumption against them, but the
strongest presumption in favor of their appearance. But
whether voices were heard in the sky, or not; whether his
mother or his father dreamed that the infant man-child
was the son of Apollo; whether a swarm of bees settled
on his lips, or not; a man who could see two sides of a
thing was born. The wonderful synthesis so familiar in
nature; the upper and the under side of the medal of
Jove; the union of impossibilities, which reappears in
every object; its real and its ideal power,—was now also
transferred entire to the consciousness of a man.

The balanced soul came. If he loved abstract truth,
he saved himself by propounding the most popular of all
principles, the absolute good, which rules rulers, and
judges the judge. If he made transcendental distinctions,
he fortified himself by drawing all his illustrations from
sources disdained by orators and polite conversers; from
mares and puppies; from pitchers and soup-ladles; from
cooks and criers; the shops of potters, horse-doctors,
butchers, and fishmongers. He cannot forgive in himself

a partiality, but is resolved that the two poles of thought shall appear in his statement. His argument and his sentence are self-poised and spherical. The two poles appear; yes, and become two hands, to grasp and appropriate their own.

Every great artist has been such by synthesis. Our strength is transitional, alternating; or, shall I say, a thread of two strands. The sea-shore, sea seen from shore, shore seen from sea; the taste of two metals in contact; and our enlarged powers at the approach and at the departure of a friend; the experience of poetic creativeness, which is not found in staying at home, nor yet in travelling, but in transitions from one to the other, which must therefore be adroitly managed to present as much transitional surface as possible; this command of two elements must explain the power and the charm of Plato. Art expresses the one, or the same by the different. Thought seeks to know unity in unity; poetry to show it by variety; that is, always by an object or symbol. Plato keeps the two vases, one of aether and one of pigment, at his side, and invariably uses both. Things added to things, as statistics, civil history, are inventories. Things used as language are inexhaustibly attractive. Plato turns incessantly the obverse and the reverse of the medal of Jove.

To take an example:—The physical philosophers had sketched each his theory of the world; the theory of atoms, of fire, of flux, of spirit; theories mechanical and chemical in their genius. Plato, a master of mathematics, studious of all natural laws and causes, feels these, as second causes, to be no theories of the world, but bare inventories and lists. To the study of nature he therefore prefixes the dogma,—"Let us declare the cause which led the Supreme Ordainer to produce and compose the universe. He was good; and he who is good has no kind of

envy. Exempt from envy, he wished that all things
should be as much as possible like himself. Whosoever,
taught by wise men, shall admit this as the prime cause
of the origin and foundation of the world, will be in the
truth." "All things are for the sake of the good, and it is
the cause of every thing beautiful." This dogma animates
and impersonates his philosophy.

The synthesis which makes the character of his mind
appears in all his talents. Where there is great compass of
wit, we usually find excellencies that combine easily in
the living man, but in description appear incompatible.
The mind of Plato is not to be exhibited by a Chinese
catalogue, but is to be apprehended by an original mind
in the exercise of its original power. In him the freest
abandonment is united with the precision of a geometer.
His daring imagination gives him the more solid grasp of
facts; as the birds of highest flight have the strongest alar
bones. His patrician polish, his intrinsic elegance, edged
by an irony so subtle that it stings and paralyses, adorn
the soundest health and strength of frame. According to
the old sentence, "If Jove should descend to the earth, he
would speak in the style of Plato."

With this palatial air, there is, for the direct aim of
several of his works, and running through the tenor of
them all, a certain earnestness, which mounts, in the
Republic, and in the Phaedo, to piety. He has been
charged with feigning sickness at the time of the death of
Socrates. But the anecdotes that have come down from
the times attest his manly interference before the people
in his master's behalf, since even the savage cry of the
assembly to Plato is preserved; and the indignation
towards popular government, in many of his pieces,
expresses a personal exasperation. He has a probity, a
native reverence for justice and honor, and a humanity

which makes him tender for the superstitions of the people. Add to this, he believes that poetry, prophecy, and the high insight, are from a wisdom of which man is not master; that the gods never philosophise; but, by a celestial mania, these miracles are accomplished. Horsed on these winged steeds, he sweeps the dim regions, visits worlds which flesh cannot enter; he saw the souls in pain; he hears the doom of the judge; he beholds the penal metempsychosis; the Fates, with the rock and shears; and hears the intoxicating hum of their spindle.

But his circumspection never forsook him. One would say he had read the inscription on the gates of Busyrane,—"Be bold;" and on the second gate,—"Be bold, be bold, and evermore be bold:" and then again had paused well at the third gate,—"Be not too bold." His strength is like the momentum of a falling planet; and his discretion, the return of its due and perfect curve,—so excellent is his Greek love of boundary, and his skill in definition. In reading logarithms, one is not more secure, than in following Plato in his flights. Nothing can be colder than his head, when the lightnings of his imagination are playing in the sky. He has finished his thinking, before he brings it to the reader; and he abounds in the surprises of a literary master. He has that opulence which furnishes, at every turn, the precise weapon he needs. As the rich man wears no more garments, drives no more horses, sits in no more chambers, than the poor,—but has that one dress, or equipage, or instrument, which is fit for the hour and the need; so Plato, in his plenty, is never restricted, but has the fit word. There is, indeed, no weapon in all the armory of wit which he did not possess and use,—epic, analysis, mania, intuition, music, satire, and irony, down to the customary and polite. His illustrations are poetry, and his jests illustrations. Socrates' profession of obstetric art is good philosophy; and his finding that word "cookery," and "adulatory art," for rhetoric, in the Gorgias, does us a substantial service still. No orator can measure in effect with him who can give good nicknames.

What moderation, and understatement, and checking his thunder in mid volley! He has good-naturedly furnished the courtier and citizen with all that can be said against the schools. "For philosophy is an elegant thing, if any one modestly meddles with it; but, if he is conversant with it more than is becoming, it corrupts the man." He could well afford to be generous,—he, who from the sunlike centrality and reach of his vision, had a faith without cloud. Such as his perception, was his speech: he plays with the doubt, and makes the most of it: he paints and quibbles; and by and by comes a sentence that moves the sea and land. The admirable earnest comes not only at intervals, in the perfect yes and no of the dialogue, but in bursts of light. "I, therefore, Callicles, am persuaded by these accounts, and consider how I may exhibit my soul before the judge in a healthy condition. Wherefore, disregarding the honors that most men value, and looking to the truth, I shall endeavor in reality to live as virtuously as I can; and, when I die, to die so. And I invite all other men, to the utmost of my power; and you, too, I in turn invite to this contest, which, I affirm, surpasses all contests here."

He is a great average man; one who, to the best thinking, adds a proportion and equality in his faculties, so that men see in him their own dreams and glimpses made available, and made to pass for what they are. A great commonsense is his warrant and qualification to be the world's interpreter. He has reason, as all the philosophic and poetic class have: but he has, also, what they have not,—this strong solving sense to reconcile his poetry with the appearances of the world, and build a bridge from the streets of cities to the Atlantis. He omits never this graduation, but slopes his thought, however picturesque the precipice on one side, to an access from the plain. He never writes in ecstasy, or catches us up into poetic raptures.

Plato apprehended the cardinal facts. He could prostrate himself on the earth, and cover his eyes, whilst he adored that which cannot be numbered, or gauged, or known, or named: that of which every thing can be affirmed and denied: that "which is entity and nonentity." He called it super-essential. He even stood ready, as in the Parmenides, to demonstrate that it was so,—that this Being exceeded the limits of intellect. No man ever more fully acknowledged the Ineffable. Having paid his homage, as for the human race, to the Illimitable, he then stood erect, and for the human race affirmed, 'And yet things are knowable!'—that is, the Asia in his mind was first heartily honored,—the ocean of love and power, before form, before will, before knowledge, the Same, the Good, the One; and now, refreshed and empowered by this worship, the instinct of Europe, namely, culture, returns; and he cries, Yet things are knowable! They are knowable, because, being from one, things correspond. There is a scale: and the correspondence of heaven to earth, of matter to mind, of the part to the whole, is our guide. As there is a science of stars, called astronomy; a science of quantities, called mathematics; a science of qualities, called chemistry; so there is a science of sciences,—I call it Dialectic,—which is the Intellect discriminating the false and the true. It rests on the observation of identity and diversity; for, to judge, is to unite to an object the notion which belongs to it. The sciences, even the best,—mathematics and astronomy,—are like sportsmen, who seize whatever prey offers, even without being able to make any use of it. Dialectic must teach the use of them. "This is of that rank that no intellectual man will enter on any study for its own sake, but only with a view to advance himself in that one sole science which embraces all."

"The essence or peculiarity of man is to comprehend a whole; or that which, in the diversity of sensations, can be comprised under a rational unity." "The soul which has never perceived the truth, cannot pass into the human form." I announce to men the Intellect. I announce the good of being interpenetrated by the mind that made nature: this benefit, namely, that it can understand nature, which it made and maketh. Nature is good, but intellect is better: as the lawgiver is before the law-receiver. I give you joy, O sons of men! that truth is altogether wholesome; that we have hope to search out what might be the very self of everything. The misery of man is to be baulked of the sight of essence, and to be stuffed with conjectures: but the supreme good is reality; the supreme beauty is reality; and all virtue and all felicity depend on this science of the real: for courage is nothing else than knowledge: the fairest fortune that can befall man, is to be guided by his daemon to that which is truly his own. This also is the essence of justice, —to attend every one his own: nay, the notion of virtue is not to be arrived at, except through direct contemplation of the divine essence. Courage, then! for, "the persuasion that we must search that which we do not know, will render us, beyond comparison, better, braver, and more industrious, than if we thought it impossible to discover what we do not know, and useless to search for it." He secures a position not to be commanded, by his passion for reality; valuing philosophy only as it is the pleasure of conversing with real being.

Thus, full of the genius of Europe, he said, *Culture*. He saw the institutions of Sparta, and recognized more genially, one would say, than any since, the hope of education. He delighted in every accomplishment, in every graceful and useful and truthful performance; above all, in the splendors of genius and intellectual achievement. "The whole of life, O Socrates, said Glauco, is, with the wise, the measure of hearing such discourses as these." What a price he sets on the feats of talent, on the powers of Pericles, of Isocrates, of Parmenides! What price, above price, on the talents themselves! He called the several faculties, gods, in his beautiful personation. What value he gives to the art of gymnastic in education; what to geometry; what to music; what to astronomy, whose appeasing and medicinal power he celebrates! In the Timaeus he indicates the highest employment of the eyes. "By us it is asserted, that God invented and bestowed sight on us for this purpose,—that, on surveying the circles of intelligence in the heavens, we might properly employ those of our own minds, which, though disturbed when compared with the others that are uniform, are still allied to their circulations; and that, having thus learned, and being naturally possessed of a correct reasoning faculty, we might, by imitating the uniform revolutions of divinity, set right our own wanderings and blunders." And in the Republic,—"By each of these disciplines, a certain organ of the soul is both purified and reanimated, which is blinded and buried by studies of another kind; an organ better worth saving than ten thousand eyes, since truth is perceived by this alone."

He said, Culture; but he first admitted its basis, and

gave immeasurably the first place to advantages of
nature. His patrician tastes laid stress on the distinctions
of birth. In the doctrine of the organic character and dis-
position is the origin of caste. "Such as were fit to govern, into their composition the informing Deity mingled
gold: into the military, silver; iron and brass for husband-
men and artificers." The East confirms itself, in all ages,
in this faith. The Koran is explicit on this point of caste.
"Men have their metal, as of gold and silver. Those of
you who were the worthy ones in the state of ignorance,
will be the worthy ones in the state of faith, as soon as
you embrace it." Plato was not less firm. "Of the five
orders of things, only four can be taught to the generality
of men." In the Republic, he insists on the temperaments
of the youth, as first of the first.

A happier example of the stress laid on nature, is in
the dialogue with the young Theages, who wishes to
receive lessons from Socrates. Socrates declares that, if
some have grown wise by associating with him, no
thanks are due to him; but, simply, whilst they were with
him, they grew wise, not because of him; he pretends
not to know the way of it. "It is adverse to many, nor can
those be benefited by associating with me, whom the
Daemon opposes; so that it is not possible for me to live
with these. With many, however, he does not prevent me
from conversing, who yet are not at all benefited by
associating with me. Such, O Theages, is the association
with me; for, if it pleases the God, you will make great
and rapid proficiency: you will not, if he does not please.
Judge whether it is not safer to be instructed by some
one of those who have power over the benefit which
they impart to men, than by me, who benefit or not, just
as it may happen." As if he had said, 'I have no system. I
cannot be answerable for you. You will be what you

must. If there is love between us, inconceivably delicious and profitable will our intercourse be; if not, your time is lost, and you will only annoy me. I shall seem to you stupid, and the reputation I have, false. Quite above us, beyond the will of you or me, is this secret affinity or repulsion laid. All my good is magnetic, and I educate, not by lessons, but by going about my business.'

He said, Culture; he said, Nature: and he failed not to add, 'There is also the divine.' There is no thought in any mind, but it quickly tends to convert itself into a power, and organizes a huge instrumentality of means. Plato, lover of limits, loved the illimitable, saw the enlargement and nobility which come from truth itself and good itself, and attempted, as if on the part of the human intellect, once for all, to do it adequate homage, —homage fit for the immense soul to receive, and yet homage becoming the intellect to render. He said, then, 'Our faculties run out into infinity, and return to us thence. We can define but a little way; but here is a fact which will not be skipped, and which to shut our eyes upon is suicide. All things are in a scale; and, begin where we will, ascend and ascend. All things are symbolical; and what we call results are beginnings.'

A key to the method and completeness of Plato is his twice bisected line. After he has illustrated the relation between the absolute good and true, and the forms of the intelligible world, he says:—"Let there be a line cut in two unequal parts. Cut again each of these two parts,—one representing the visible, the other the intelligible world,—and these two new sections, representing the bright part and the dark part of these worlds, you will have, for one of the sections of the visible world, —images, that is, both shadows and reflections;—for the other section, the objects of these images,—that is, plants, animals, and the works of art and nature. Then divide the intelligible world in like manner; the one section will be of opinions and hypotheses, and the other section, of truths." To these four sections, the four operations of the soul correspond,—conjecture, faith, understanding, reason. As every pool reflects the image of the sun, so every thought and thing restores us an image and creature of the supreme Good. The universe is perforated by a million channels for his activity. All things mount and mount.

All his thought has this ascension; in Phaedrus, teaching that beauty is the most lovely of all things, exciting hilarity, and shedding desire and confidence through the universe, wherever it enters; and it enters, in some degree, into all things: but that there is another, which is as much more beautiful than beauty, as beauty is than chaos; namely, wisdom, which our wonderful organ of sight cannot reach unto, but which, could it be seen, would ravish us with its perfect reality. He has the same regard to it as the source of excellence in works of art. "When an artificer, in the fabrication of any work, looks to that which always subsists according *to the same*; and, employing a model of this kind, expresses its idea and power in his work; it must follow, that his production should be beautiful. But when he beholds that which is born and dies, it will be far from beautiful."

Thus ever: the Banquet is a teaching in the same spirit, familiar now to all the poetry, and to all the sermons of the world, that the love of the sexes is initial; and symbolizes, at a distance, the passion of the soul for that immense lake of beauty it exists to seek. This faith in the Divinity is never out of mind, and constitutes the limitation of all his dogmas. Body cannot teach wisdom;— God only. In the same mind, he constantly affirms that virtue cannot be taught; that it is not a science, but an inspiration; that the greatest goods are produced to us through mania, and are assigned to us by a divine gift.

This leads me to that central figure, which he has established in his Academy, as the organ through which every considered opinion shall be announced, and whose biography he has likewise so labored, that the historic facts are lost in the light of Plato's mind. Socrates and Plato are the double star, which the most powerful instruments will not entirely separate. Socrates, again, in his traits and genius, is the best example of that synthesis which constitutes Plato's extraordinary power. Socrates, a man of humble stem, but honest enough; of the commonest history; of a personal homeliness so remarkable, as to be a cause of wit in others,—the rather that his broad good nature and exquisite taste for a joke invited the sally, which was sure to be paid. The players personated him on the stage; the potters copied his ugly face on their stone jugs. He was a cool fellow, adding to his humor a perfect temper, and a knowledge of his man, be he who he might whom he talked with, which laid the companion open to certain defeat in any debate,—and in debate he immoderately delighted. The young men are prodigiously fond of him, and invite him to their feasts, whither he goes for conversation. He can drink, too; has the strongest head in Athens; and, after leaving the whole party under the table, goes away, as if nothing had happened, to begin new dialogues with somebody that is sober. In short, he was what our country-people call *an old one*.

He affected a good many citizen-like tastes, was monstrously fond of Athens, hated trees, never willingly went beyond the walls, knew the old characters, valued the bores and philistines, thought every thing in Athens a little better than anything in any other place. He was plain as a Quaker in habit and speech, affected low phrases, and illustrations from cocks and quails, soup-pans and sycamore-spoons, grooms and farriers, and unnamable offices,—especially if he talked with any superfine person. He had a Franklin-like wisdom. Thus, he showed one who was afraid to go on foot to Olympia, that it was no more than his daily walk within doors, if continuously extended, would easily reach.

Plain old uncle as he was, with his great ears,—an immense talker,—the rumor ran, that, on one or two occasions, in the war with Boeotia, he had shown a determination which had covered the retreat of a troop; and there was some story that, under cover of folly, he had, in the city government, when one day he chanced to hold a seat there, evinced a courage in opposing singly the popular voice, which had well-nigh ruined him. He is very poor; but then he is hardy as a soldier, and can live on a few olives; usually, in the strictest sense, on bread and water, except when entertained by his friends. His necessary expenses were exceedingly small, and no one could live as he did. He wore no under garment; his upper garment was the same for sum-mer and winter, and he went barefooted; and it is said that, to procure the pleasure, which he loves, of talking at his ease all day with the most elegant and cultivated young men, he will now and then return to his shop and carve statues, good or bad, for sale. However that be, it is certain that he had grown to delight in nothing else than this conversation; and that, under his hypocritical pretence of knowing nothing, he attacks and brings down all the fine speakers, all the fine philosophers of Athens, whether natives, or strangers from Asia Minor and the islands. Nobody can refuse to talk with him, he is so honest, and really curious to know; a man who was willingly confuted, if he did not speak the truth, and who willingly confuted others, asserting what was false; and not less pleased when confuted than when confuting; for he thought not any evil happened to men, of such a magnitude as false opinion respecting the just and unjust. A pitiless disputant, who knows nothing, but the bounds of whose conquering intelligence no man had ever reached; whose temper was imperturbable; whose dreadful logic was always leisurely and sportive; so careless and ignorant, as to disarm the wariest, and draw them, in the pleasantest manner, into horrible doubts and confusion. But he always knew the way out; knew it, yet would not tell it. No escape; he drives them to terrible choices by his dilemmas, and tosses the Hippiases and Gorgiases with their grand reputations, as a boy tosses his balls. The tyrannous realist!—Meno has discoursed a thousand times, at length, on virtue, before many companies, and very well, as it appeared to him; but at this moment, he cannot even tell what it is,—this cramp-fish of a Socrates has so bewitched him.

This hard-headed humorist, whose strange conceits, drollery, and *bonhommie* diverted the young patricians, whilst the rumor of his sayings and quibbles gets abroad every day, turns out, in the sequel, to have a probity as invincible as his logic, and to be either insane, or, at least, under cover of this play, enthusiastic in his religion. When accused before the judges of subverting the popular creed, he affirms the immortality of the soul, the future reward and punishment; and, refusing to recant, in a caprice of the popular government, was condemned to die, and sent to the prison. Socrates entered the prison, and took away all ignominy from the place, which could not be a prison, whilst he was there. Crito bribed the jailer; but Socrates would not go out by treachery. "Whatever inconvenience ensue, nothing is to be preferred before justice. These things I hear like pipes and drums, whose sound makes me deaf to every thing you say." The fame of this prison, the fame of the discourses there, and the drinking of the hemlock, are one of the most precious passages in the history of the world.

The rare coincidence, in one ugly body, of the droll and the martyr, the keen street and market debater with the sweetest saint known to any history at that time, had forcibly struck the mind of Plato, so capacious of these contrasts; and the figure of Socrates, by a necessity, placed itself in the foreground of the scene, as the fittest dispenser of the intellectual treasures he had to communicate. It was a rare fortune that this Aesop of the mob, and this robed scholar, should meet, to make each other immortal in the irmutual faculty. The strange synthesis, in the character of Socrates, capped the synthesis in the mind of Plato. Moreover, by this means, he was able, in the direct way, and without envy, to avail himself of the wit and weight of Socrates, to which unquestionably his own debt was great; and these derived again their principal advantage from the perfect art of Plato.

It remains to say, that the defect of Plato in power is only that which results inevitably from his quality. He is intellectual in his aim; and, therefore, in expression, literary. Mounting into heaven, diving into the pit, expounding the laws of the state, the passion of love, the remorse of crime, the hope of the parting soul,—he is literary, and never otherwise. It is almost the sole deduction from the merit of Plato, that his writings have not,—what is, no doubt, incident to this regnancy of intellect in his work,—the vital authority which the screams of prophets and the sermons of unlettered Arabs and Jews possess. There is an interval; and to cohesion, contact is necessary.

I know not what can be said in reply to this criticism, but that we have come to a fact in the nature of things: an oak is not an orange. The qualities of sugar remain with sugar, and those of salt, with salt.

In the second place, he has not a system. The dearest defenders and disciples are at fault. He attempted a theory of the universe, and his theory is not complete or self-evident. One man thinks he means this; and another, that: he has said one thing in one place, and the reverse of it in another place. He is charged with having failed to make the transition from ideas to matter. Here is the world, sound as a nut, perfect, not the smallest piece of chaos left, never a stitch nor an end, not a mark of haste, or botching, or second thought; but the theory of the world is a thing of shreds and patches.

The longest wave is quickly lost in the sea. Plato would willingly have a Platonism, a known and accurate expression for the world, and it should be accurate. It shall be the world passed through the mind of Plato,— nothing less. Every atom shall have the Platonic tinge; every atom, every relation or quality you knew before, you shall know again, and find here, but now ordered; not nature, but art. And you shall feel that Alexander indeed overran, with men and horses, some countries of the planet; but countries, and things of which countries are made, elements, planet itself, laws of planet and of men, have passed through this man as bread into his body, and become no longer bread, but body: so all this mammoth morsel has become Plato. He has clapped copyright on the world. This is the ambition of individualism. But the mouthful proves too large. *Boa constrictor* has good will to eat it, but he is foiled. He falls abroad in

the attempt; and biting, gets strangled: the bitten world
holds the biter fast by his own teeth. There he perishes:
unconquered nature lives on, and forgets him. So it fares
with all: so must it fare with Plato. In view of eternal
nature, Plato turns out to be philosophical exercitations.
He argues on this side, and on that. The acutest German,
the lovingest disciple, could never tell what Platonism
was; indeed, admirable texts can be quoted on both
sides of every great question from him.

These things we are forced to say, if we must consider the effort of Plato, or of any philosopher, to dispose
of Nature,—which will not be disposed of. No power of
genius has ever yet had the smallest success in explaining existence. The perfect enigma remains. But there is
an injustice in assuming this ambition for Plato. Let us
not seem to treat with flippancy his venerable name.
Men, in proportion to their intellect, have admitted his
transcendent claims. The way to know him, is to compare him, not with nature, but with other men. How
many ages have gone by, and he remains unapproached!
A chief structure of human wit, like Karnac, or the medi-
aeval cathedrals, or the Etrurian remains, it requires all
the breath of human faculty to know it. I think it is trueli-
est seen, when seen with the most respect. His sense
deepens, his merits multiply, with study. When we say,
here is a fine collection of fables; or, when we praise the
style; or, the common sense; or arithmetic; we speak as
boys, and much of our impatient criticism of the dialectic, I suspect, is no better.

The criticism is like our impatience of miles, when
we are in a hurry; but it is still best that a mile should
have seventeen hundred and sixty yards. The great-eyed
Plato proportioned the lights and shades after the genius
of our life.

Plato: New Readings

The publication, in Mr. Bohn's "Serial Library," of the excellent translations of Plato, which we esteem one of the chief benefits the cheap press has yielded, gives us an occasion to take hastily a few more notes of the elevation and bearings of this fixed star; or, to add a bulletin, like the journals, of *Plato at the latest dates*.

Modern science, by the extent of its generalization, has learned to indemnify the student of man for the defects of individuals, by tracing growth and ascent in races; and, by the simple expedient of lighting up the vast background, generates a feeling of complacency and hope. The human being has the saurian and the plant in his rear. His arts and sciences, the easy issue of his brain, look glorious when prospectively beheld from the distant brain of ox, crocodile and fish. It seems as if nature, in regarding the geologic night behind her, when, in five or six millenniums, she had turned out five or six men, as Homer, Phidias, Menu and Columbus, was no wise discontented with the result. These samples attested the virtue of the tree. These were a clear amelioration of trilobite and saurus, and a good basis for further proceeding. With this artist, time and space are cheap, and she is insensible to what you say of tedious preparation. She waited tranquilly the flowing periods of paleontology, for the hour to be struck when man should arrive. Then periods must pass before the motion of the earth can be suspected; then before the map of the instincts and the cultivable powers can be drawn. But as of races, so the succession of individual men is fatal and beautiful, and Plato has the fortune in the history of mankind to mark an epoch.

Plato's fame does not stand on a syllogism, or on any masterpieces of the Socratic reasoning, or on any thesis, as for example, the immortality of the soul. He is more than an expert, or a schoolman, or a geometer, or the prophet of a peculiar message. He represents the privilege of the intellect, the power, namely, of carrying up every fact to successive, platforms, and so disclosing, in every fact, a germ of expansion. These expansions are in the essence of thought. The naturalist would never help us to them by any discoveries of the extent of the universe, but is as poor, when cataloguing the resolved nebula of Orion, as when measuring the angles of an acre. But the Republic of Plato, by these expansions, may be said to require, and so to anticipate, the astronomy of Laplace. The expansions are organic. The mind does not create what it perceives, any more than the eye creates the rose. In ascribing to Plato the merit of announcing them, we only say, here was a more complete man, who could apply to nature the whole scale of the senses, the understanding, and the reason. These expansions, or extensions, consist in continuing the spiritual sight where the horizon falls on our natural vision, and, by this second sight, discovering the long lines of law which shoot in every direction. Everywhere he stands on a path which has no end, but runs continuously round the universe. Therefore, every word becomes an exponent of nature. Whatever he looks upon discloses a second sense, and ulterior senses. His perception of the generation of contraries, of death out of life, and life out of death,—that law by which, in nature, decomposition is recomposition, and putrefaction and cholera are only signals of a new creation; his discernment of the little in the large, and the large in the small; studying the state in the citizen, and the citizen, in the state; and leaving it doubt-

ful whether he exhibited the Republic as an allegory on
the education of the private soul; his beautiful definitions
of ideas, of time, of form, of figure, of the line, sometimes hypothetically given, as his defining of virtue,
courage, justice, temperance; his love of the apologue,
and his apologues themselves; the cave of Trophonius;
the ring of Gyges; the charioteer and two horses; the
golden, silver, brass, and iron temperaments; Theuth and
Thamus; and the visions of Hades and the Fates,—fables
which have imprinted themselves in the human memory
like the signs of the zodiac; his soliform eye and his
boniform soul; his doctrine of assimilation; his doctrine
of reminiscence; his clear vision of the laws of return, or
reaction, which secure instant justice throughout the universe, instanced everywhere, but specially in the doctrine, "what comes from God to us, returns from us to
God," and in Socrates' belief that the laws below are sis-
ters of the laws above.

More striking examples are his moral conclusions.
Plato affirms the coincidence of science and virtue; for
vice can never know itself and virtue; but virtue knows
both itself and vice. The eye attested that justice was
best, as long as it was profitable; Plato affirms that it is
profitable throughout; that the profit is intrinsic, though
the just conceal his justice from gods and men; that it is
better to suffer injustice, than to do it; that the sinner
ought to covet punishment; that the lie was more hurtful
than homicide; and that ignorance, or the involuntary lie,
was more calamitous than involuntary homicide; that the
soul is unwillingly deprived of true opinions; and that no
man sins willingly; that the order or proceeding of nature
was from the mind to the body; and, though a sound
body cannot restore an unsound mind, yet a good soul
can, by its virtue, render the body the best possible. The

intelligent have a right over the ignorant, namely, the right of instructing them. The right punishment of one out of tune is to make him play in tune, the fine which the good, refusing to govern, ought to pay, is, to be governed by a worse man; that his guards shall not handle gold and silver, but shall be instructed that there is gold and silver in their souls, which will make men willing to give them every thing which they need.

This second sight explains the stress laid on geometry. He saw that the globe of earth was not more lawful and precise than was the super-sensible; that a celestial geometry was in place there, as a logic of lines and angles here below; that the world was throughout mathematical; the proportions are constant of oxygen, azote, and lime; there is just so much water, and slate, and magnesia; not less are the proportions constant of the moral elements.

This eldest Goethe, hating varnish and falsehood, delighted in revealing the real at the base of the accidental; in discovering connection, continuity, and representation, everywhere; hating insulation; and appears like the god of wealth among the cabins of vagabonds, opening power and capability in everything he touches. Ethical science was new and vacant, when Plato could write thus: —"Of all whose arguments are left to the men of the present time, no one has ever yet condemned injustice, or praised justice, otherwise than as respects the repute, honors, and emoluments arising therefrom; while, as respects either of them in itself, and subsisting by its own power in the soul of the possessor, and concealed both from gods and men, no one has yet sufficiently investigated, either in poetry or prose writings, —how, namely, that the one is the greatest of all the evils that the soul has within it, and justice the greatest good."

His definition of ideas, as what is simple, permanent, uniform, and self-existent, forever discriminating them from the notions of the understanding, marks an era in the world. He was born to behold the self-evolving power of spirit, endless generator of new ends; a power which is the key at once to the centrality and the evanescence of things. Plato is so centred, that he can well spare all his dogmas. Thus the fact of knowledge and ideas reveals to him the fact of eternity; and the doctrine of reminiscence he offers as the most probable particular explication. Call that fanciful,—it matters not: the connection between our knowledge and the abyss of being is still real, and the explication must be not less magnificent.

He has indicated every eminent point in speculation. He wrote on the scale of the mind itself, so that all things have symmetry in his tablet. He put in all the past, without weariness, and descended into detail with a courage like that he witnessed in nature. One would say, that his forerunners had mapped out each a farm, or a district, or an island, in intellectual geography, but that Plato first drew the sphere. He domesticates the soul in nature: man is the microcosm. All the circles of the visible heaven represent as many circles in the rational soul. There is no lawless particle, and there is nothing casual in the action of the human mind. The names of things, too, are fatal, following the nature of things. All the gods of the Pantheon are, by their names, significant of a profound sense. The gods are the ideas. Pan is speech, or manifestation; Saturn, the contemplative; Jove, the regal soul; and Mars, passion. Venus is proportion; Calliope, the soul of the world; Aglaia, intellectual illustration.

These thoughts, in sparkles of light, had appeared often to pious and to poetic souls; but this well-bred, all-knowing Greek geometer comes with command, gathers them all up into rank and gradation, the Euclid of holiness, and marries the two parts of nature. Before all men, he saw the intellectual values of the moral sentiment. He describes his own ideal, when he paints in Timaeus a god leading things from disorder into order. He kindled a fire so truly in the centre, that we see the sphere illuminated, and can distinguish poles, equator, and lines of latitude, every arc and node: a theory so averaged, so modulated, that you would say, the winds of ages had swept through this rhythmic structure, and not that it was the brief extempore blotting of one short-lived scribe. Hence it has happened that a very well-marked class of souls, namely, those who delight in giving a spiritual, that is, an ethico-intellectual expression to every truth, by exhibiting an ulterior end which is yet legitimate to it, are said to Platonise. Thus, Michel Angelo is a Platonist, in his sonnets. Shakspeare is a Platonist, when he writes,

> "Nature is made better by no mean,
> but nature makes that mean,"

or,

> "He, that can endure
> To follow with allegiance a fallen lord,
> Does conquer him that did his master conquer,
> And earns a place in the story."

Hamlet is a pure Platonist, and 'tis the magnitude only of Shakspeare's proper genius that hinders him from being classed as the most eminent of this school. Swedenborg, throughout his prose poem of "Conjugal Love," is a Platonist.

His subtlety commended him to men of thought. The secret of his popular success is the moral aim, which endeared him to mankind. "Intellect," he said, "is king of heaven and of earth;" but, in Plato, intellect is always moral. His writings have also the sempiternal youth of poetry. For their arguments, most of them, might have been couched in sonnets: and poetry has never soared higher than in the Timaeus and the Phaedrus. As the poet, too, he is only contemplative. He did not, like Pythagoras, break himself with an institution. All his painting in the Republic must be esteemed mythical, with intent to bring out, sometimes in violent colors, his thought. You cannot institute, without peril of charlatanism.

It was a high scheme, his absolute privilege for the best (which, to make emphatic, he expressed by community of women,) as the premium which he would set on grandeur. There shall be exempts of two kinds: first, those who by demerit have put themselves below protection,—outlaws; and secondly, those who by eminence of nature and desert are out of the reach of your rewards. Let such be free of the city, and above the law. We confide them to themselves; let them do with us as they will. Let none presume to measure the irregularities of Michel Angelo and Socrates by village scales.

In his eighth book of the Republic, he throws a little mathematical dust in our eyes. I am sorry to see him, after such noble superiorities, permitting the lie to governors. Plato plays Providence a little with the baser sort, as people allow themselves with their dogs and cats.

The Essay
"Compensation"

In his essay on Plato, Emerson divided the philosophical world into two components, the One and the Many, or Unity and Diversity, and said that it was Plato's genius to encompass both. In "Compensation," with similar powers of compression, Emerson draws upon the dynamics of polarity, or the laws of action and reaction, to define justice, or the laws of compensation. It is a challenging essay because we are accustomed to thinking very differently about matters of justice in our daily lives.

In the *Republic* (363), Plato describes an ancient Orphic doctrine of justice in which those who are just in their earthly lives are given in heaven an existence of feasting and drunkenness, while the unjust in this life, who presumably feast and drink to their heart's content, are confined to mud and made to carry water in sieves. As Emerson phrases it in this essay, the Good say to the Bad, "You sin now; we shall sin by and by; we would sin now if we could; not being successful, we expect our revenge tomorrow." This simplistic understanding of justice is both unnatural and banal. Emerson's intent is to put justice on a natural and spiritual footing.

This essay allows us to reach an understanding of

Emerson's view of evil. Even though the essay declares, "Every thing has two sides, a good and an evil," Emerson's long view was that evil is not a distinct force in opposition to the Good, but is rather privation, the absence of Good, as cold is the absence of heat. Evil is equated to ignorance, the absence of awareness. This absence may well be malignant, as in crimes of genocide and the conscious taking of a human life, but the fact remains that such malignancy comes from an absence of good, not from inherent evil. As Emerson says, "The history of persecution is a history of endeavors to cheat nature, to make water run up hill, to twist a rope of sand." Evil, then, is a result of separation, isolation, and ignorance.

Emerson's idealism always penetrates the surfaces of an argument, finding in the most bleak of circumstances or most malignant of actions a compensation. We can look at modern experience to see how the principle applies. In the twentieth century no greater evil than the Holocaust has confronted our sense of fundamental justice. How can there be any justice in the face of such misery and evil? Some Jewish philosophers have claimed that the Holocaust affirmed the death of God. Others suggest that humanity no longer has a right to survive as a species as a result of the events which took place in Europe from 1938 to 1945.

Aside from Emerson's consolations of time as healer of these deep wounds, there is his more fundamental view that the world is soul, not circumstance, and that the ultimate fact of life is Being itself. As such, "all actions are indifferent," in the sense not of emotional indifference, or uncaring, but of an indifferency based on balance, a justice that keeps a perfect sway on events and circumstances. The Holocaust overwhelmed us as a

fact. If history, as Emerson believed, is the record of the
collective human mind, then the Holocaust must find its
meaning in the workings of that mind. If the events so
appalling to our collective conscience remain in isolation,
we fail to witness with the same conscience the life-
affirming aftermath as part of the record of mind as well.
Forces of horror have always emerged from the darkness
of ignorance and isolation to plague us. This is part of
the sleep that drugs our awareness, but it does not deny
the light. There remains a latent power which arises in
moments of great need. But the question persists, as it
did also for Emerson, why the power to overwhelm
this darkness seems so latent, why, as he asked in
"Experience," ". . . did our birth fall in some fit of indigence and frugality in nature. . . ." It appears that this
planet is a tough place for the development of consciousness, but as Robert Frost put it, "The Earth's the
right place for love; I don't know where it's likely to go
better."

When we ask in the midst of tragedy, "Why has God
allowed this to happen?" the answer lies in the nature of
God as wholeness, "swallowing up all relations, parts
and times, within itself." In our pain, overwhelming as it
is, we often feel separate, isolated, and victimized. Loss
teaches a great lesson; we are separate only when we
identify ourselves with the loss. It is not that God's plan
is too obscure for our understanding, but rather that our
understanding of God is too narrow for the circumstances, especially when we are isolated by our grief.

Expansion is always the proper response to circumstances. In the human realm love is the means of such
expansion, not intellectual grasping. In Emerson's life,
loss was a regular occurrence. Death took his father, his
young wife Ellen, his son Waldo, and his brothers

Edward and Charles, all when they were young. These losses caused him to constrict his being for a time, overwhelming his essential optimism, but since optimism is merely a superficial emotional stance and easily shattered, a more substantial and fundamental anchor was needed for his existence. His idealism (which is not the same as optimism) was never more practical than in these moments of personal loss, and it allowed him passage to recovery.

COMPENSATION

The wings of Time are black and white,
Pied with morning and with night.
Mountain tall and ocean deep
Trembling balance duly keep.
In changing moon, in tidal wave,
Glows the feud of Want and Have.
Gauge of more and less through space
Electric star and pencil plays.
The lonely Earth amid the balls
That hurry through the eternal halls,
A makeweight flying to the void,
Supplemental asteroid,
Or compensatory spark,
Shoots across the neutral Dark.

Man's the elm, and Wealth the vine;
Stanch and strong the tendrils twine:
Though the frail ringlets thee deceive,
None from its stock that vine can reave.
Fear not, then, thou child infirm,
There's no god dare wrong a worm.

Laurel crowns cleave to deserts,
And power to him who power exerts;
Hast not thy share? On winged feet,
Lo! it rushes thee to meet;
And all that Nature made thy own,
Floating in air or pent in stone,
Will rive the hills and swim the sea,
And, like thy shadow, follow thee.

Ever since I was a boy, I have wished to write a discourse on Compensation: for it seemed to me when very young, that on this subject life was ahead of theology, and the people knew more than the preachers taught. The documents, too, from which the doctrine is to be drawn, charmed my fancy by their endless variety, and lay always before me, even in sleep; for they are the tools in our hands, the bread in our basket, the transactions of the street, the farm, and the dwelling-house, greetings, relations, debts and credits, the influence of character, the nature and endowment of all men. It seemed to me, also, that in it might be shown men a ray of divinity, the present action of the soul of this world, clean from all vestige of tradition, and so the heart of man might be bathed by an inundation of eternal love, conversing with that which he knows was always and always must be, because it really is now. It appeared, moreover, that if this doctrine could be stated in terms with any resemblance to those bright intuitions in which this truth is sometimes revealed to us, it would be a star in many dark hours and crooked passages in our journey that would not suffer us to lose our way.

I was lately confirmed in these desires by hearing a sermon at church. The preacher, a man esteemed for his orthodoxy, unfolded in the ordinary manner the doctrine of the Last Judgment. He assumed, that judgment is not executed in this world; that the wicked are successful; that the good are miserable; and then urged from reason and from Scripture a compensation to be made to both parties in the next life. No offence appeared to be taken by the congregation at this doctrine. As far as I could observe, when the meeting broke up, they separated without remark on the sermon.

Yet what was the import of this teaching? What did the preacher mean by saying that the good are miserable in the present life? Was it that houses and lands, offices, wine, horses, dress, luxury, are had by unprincipled men, whilst the saints are poor and despised; and that a compensation is to be made to these last hereafter, by giving them the like gratifications another day,—bank-stock and doubloons, venison and champagne? This must be the compensation intended; for what else? Is it that they are to have leave to pray and praise? to love and serve men? Why, that they can do now. The legitimate inference the disciple would draw was,—'We are to have *such* a good time as the sinners have now';—or, to push it to its extreme import,—'You sin now; we shall sin by and by; we would sin now, if we could; not being successful, we expect our revenge to-morrow.'

The fallacy lay in the immense concession, that the bad are successful; that justice is not done now. The blindness of the preacher consisted in deferring to the base estimate of the market of what constitutes a manly success, instead of confronting and convicting the world from the truth; announcing the presence of the soul; the omnipotence of the will: and so establishing the standard of good and ill, of success and falsehood.

I find a similar base tone in the popular religious works of the day, and the same doctrines assumed by the

literary men when occasionally they treat the related top-
ics. I think that our popular theology has gained in decorum, and not in principle, over the superstitions it has
displaced. But men are better than this theology. Their
daily life gives it the lie. Every ingenuous and aspiring
soul leaves the doctrine behind him in his own experience; and all men feel sometimes the falsehood which
they cannot demonstrate. For men are wiser than they
know. That which they hear in schools and pulpits without after-thought, if said in conversation, would probably
be questioned in silence. If a man dogmatize in a mixed
company on Providence and the divine laws, he is
answered by a silence which conveys well enough to an
observer the dissatisfaction of the hearer, but his incapac-
ity to make his own statement.

I shall attempt in this and the following chapter to
record some facts that indicate the path of the law of
Compensation; happy beyond my expectation, if I shall
truly draw the smallest arc of this circle.

POLARITY, or action and reaction, we meet in every
part of nature; in darkness and light; in heat and cold; in
the ebb and flow of waters; in male and female; in the
inspiration and expiration of plants and animals; in the
equation of quantity and quality in the fluids of the animal body; in the systole and diastole of the heart; in the
undulations of fluids, and of sound; in the centrifugal
and centripetal gravity; in electricity, galvanism, and
chemical affinity. Superinduce magnetism at one end of a
needle; the opposite magnetism takes place at the other
end. If the south attracts, the north repels. To empty
here, you must condense there. An inevitable dualism
bisects nature, so that each thing is a half, and suggests
another thing to make it whole; as, spirit, matter; man,

woman; odd, even; subjective, objective; in, out; upper, under; motion, rest; yea, nay.

Whilst the world is thus dual, so is every one of its parts. The entire system of things gets represented in every particle. There is somewhat that resembles the ebb and flow of the sea, day and night, man and woman, in a single needle of the pine, in a kernel of corn, in each individual of every animal tribe. The reaction, so grand in the elements, is repeated within these small boundaries. For example, in the animal kingdom the physiologist has observed that no creatures are favorites, but a certain compensation balances every gift and every defect. A surplusage given to one part is paid out of a reduction from another part of the same creature. If the head and neck are enlarged, the trunk and extremities are cut short.

The theory of the mechanic forces is another example. What we gain in power is lost in time; and the converse. The periodic or compensating errors of the planets is another instance. The influences of climate and soil in political history are another. The cold climate invigorates. The barren soil does not breed fevers, crocodiles, tigers, or scorpions.

The same dualism underlies the nature and condition of man. Every excess causes a defect; every defect an excess. Every sweet hath its sour; every evil its good. Every faculty which is a receiver of pleasure has an equal penalty put on its abuse. It is to answer for its moderation with its life. For every grain of wit there is a grain of folly. For every thing you have missed, you have gained something else; and for every thing you gain, you lose something. If riches increase, they are increased that use them. If the gatherer gathers too much, nature takes out of the man what she puts into his chest; swells the estate, but kills the owner. Nature hates monopolies and exceptions. The waves of the sea do not more speedily seek a level from their loftiest tossing, than the varieties of condition tend to equalize themselves. There is always some levelling circumstance that puts down the overbearing, the strong, the rich, the fortunate, substantially on the same ground with all others. Is a man too strong and fierce for society, and by temper and position a bad citizen,—a morose ruffian, with a dash of the pirate in him;—nature sends him a troop of pretty sons and daughters, who are getting along in the dame's classes at the village school, and love and fear for them smoothes his grim scowl to courtesy. Thus she contrives to intenerate the granite and feldspar, takes the boar out and puts the lamb in, and keeps her balance true.

The farmer imagines power and place are fine things. But the President has paid dear for his White House. It has commonly cost him all his peace, and the best of his manly attributes. To preserve for a short time so conspicuous an appearance before the world, he is content to eat dust before the real masters who stand erect behind the throne. Or, do men desire the more substantial and permanent grandeur of genius? Neither has this an immunity. He who by force of will or of thought is great, and overlooks thousands, has the charges of that eminence. With every influx of light comes new danger. Has he light? he must bear witness to the light, and always outrun that sympathy which gives him such keen satisfaction, by his fidelity to new revelations of the incessant soul. He must hate father and mother, wife and child. Has he all that the world loves and admires and covets?—he must cast behind him their admiration, and afflict them by faithfulness to his truth, and become a byword and a hissing.

This law writes the laws of cities and nations. It is in

vain to build or plot or combine against it. Things refuse to be mismanaged long. *Res nolunt diu male administrari*. Though no checks to a new evil appear, the checks exist, and will appear. If the government is cruel, the governor's life is not safe. If you tax too high, the revenue will yield nothing. If you make the criminal code sanguinary, juries will not convict. If the law is too mild, private vengeance comes in. If the government is a terrific democracy, the pressure is resisted by an overcharge of energy in the citizen, and life glows with a fiercer flame. The true life and satisfactions of man seem to elude the utmost rigors or felicities of condition, and to establish themselves with great indifference under all varieties of circumstances. Under all governments the influence of character remains the same,—in Turkey and in New England about alike. Under the primeval despots of Egypt, history honestly confesses that man must have been as free as culture could make him.

These appearances indicate the fact that the universe is represented in every one of its particles. Every thing in nature contains all the powers of nature. Every thing is made of one hidden stuff; as the naturalist sees one type under every metamorphosis, and regards a horse as a running man, a fish as a swimming man, a bird as a flying man, a tree as a rooted man. Each new form repeats not only the main character of the type, but part for part all the details, all the aims, furtherances, hindrances, energies, and whole system of every other. Every occupation, trade, art, transaction, is a compend of the world, and a correlative of every other. Each one is an entire emblem of human life; of its good and ill, its trials, its enemies, its course and its end. And each one must somehow accommodate the whole man, and recite all his destiny.

The world globes itself in a drop of dew. The microscope cannot find the animalcule which is less perfect for being little. Eyes, ears, taste, smell, motion, resistance, appetite, and organs of reproduction that take hold on eternity,—all find room to consist in the small creature. So do we put our life into every act. The true doctrine of omnipresence is, that God reappears with all his parts in every moss and cobweb. The value of the universe contrives to throw itself into every point. If the good is there, so is the evil; if the affinity, so the repulsion; if the force, so the limitation.

Thus is the universe alive. All things are moral. That soul, which within us is a sentiment, outside of us is a law. We feel its inspiration; out there in history we can see its fatal strength. "It is in the world, and the world was made by it." Justice is not postponed. A perfect equity adjusts its balance in all parts of life. (*Oi chusoi Dios aei enpiptousi*),—The dice of God are always loaded. The world looks like a multiplication-table, or a mathematical equation, which, turn it how you will, balances itself. Take what figure you will, its exact value, nor more nor less, still returns to you. Every secret is told, every crime is punished, every virtue rewarded, every wrong redressed, in silence and certainty. What we call retribution is the universal necessity by which the whole appears wherever a part appears. If you see smoke, there must be fire. If you see a hand or a limb, you know that the trunk to which it belongs is there behind.

Every act rewards itself, or, in other words, integrates itself, in a twofold manner; first, in the thing, or in real nature; and secondly, in the circumstance, or in apparent nature. Men call the circumstance the retribution. The causal retribution is in the thing, and is seen by the soul. The retribution in the circumstance is seen by the understanding; it is inseparable from the thing, but is often spread over a long time, and so does not become distinct until after many years. The specific stripes may follow late after the offence, but they follow because they accompany it. Crime and punishment grow out of one stem. Punishment is a fruit that unsus pected ripens within the flower of the pleasure which concealed it. Cause and effect, means and ends, seed and fruit, cannot be severed; for the effect already blooms in the cause, the end preexists in the means, the fruit in the seed.

Whilst thus the world will be whole, and refuses to be disparted, we seek to act partially, to sunder, to appropriate; for example,—to gratify the senses, we sever the pleasure of the senses from the needs of the character. The ingenuity of man has always been dedicated to the solution of one problem,—how to detach the sensual sweet, the sensual strong, the sensual bright, etc., from the moral sweet, the moral deep, the moral fair; that is, again, to contrive to cut clean off this upper surface so thin as to leave it bottomless; to get a *one end*, without an *other end*. The soul says, Eat; the body would feast. The soul says, The man and woman shall be one flesh and one soul; the body would join the flesh only. The soul says, Have dominion over all things to the ends of virtue; the body would have the power over things to its own ends.

The soul strives amain to live and work through all things. It would be the only fact. All things shall be added unto it,—power, pleasure, knowledge, beauty. The particular man aims to be somebody; to set up for himself; to truck and higgle for a private good; and, in particulars, to ride, that he may ride; to dress, that he may be dressed; to eat, that he may eat; and to govern, that he may be seen. Men seek to be great; they would have offices, wealth, power, and fame. They think that to be great is to possess one side of nature,—the sweet, without the other side,—the bitter.

This dividing and detaching is steadily counteracted. Up to this day, it must be owned, no projector has had the smallest success. The parted water reunites behind our hand. Pleasure is taken out of pleasant things, profit out of profitable things, power out of strong things, as soon as we seek to separate them from the whole. We can no more halve things and get the sensual good, by itself, than we can get an inside that shall have no outside, or a light without a shadow. "Drive out nature with a fork, she comes running back."

Life invests itself with inevitable conditions, which the unwise seek to dodge, which one and another brags that he does not know; that they do not touch him;—but the brag is on his lips, the conditions are in his soul. If he escapes them in one part, they attack him in another more vital part. If he has escaped them in form, and in the appearance, it is because he has resisted his life, and fled from himself, and the retribution is so much death. So signal is the failure of all attempts to make this separation of the good from the tax, that the experiment would not be tried,—since to try it is to be mad,—but for the circumstance, that when the disease began in the will, of rebellion and separation, the intellect is at once infected, so that the man ceases to see God whole in each object, but is able to see the sensual allurement of an object, and not see the sensual hurt; he sees the mermaid's head, but not the dragon's tail; and thinks he can cut off that which he would have, from that which he would not have. "How secret art thou who dwellest in the highest heavens in silence, O thou only great God, sprinkling with an unwearied Providence certain penal blindnesses upon such as have unbridled desires!"

The human soul is true to these facts in the painting of fable, of history, of law, of proverbs, of conversation. It finds a tongue in literature unawares. Thus the Greeks called Jupiter, Supreme Mind; but having traditionally ascribed to him many base actions, they involuntarily made amends to reason, by tying up the hands of so bad a god. He is made as helpless as a king of England. Prometheus knows one secret which Jove must bargain for; Minerva, another. He cannot get his own thunders; Minerva keeps the key of them.

> "Of all the gods, I only know the keys
> That ope the solid doors within whose vaults
> His thunders sleep."

A plain confession of the in-working of the All, and of its moral aim. The Indian mythology ends in the same ethics; and it would seem impossible for any fable to be invented and get any currency which was not moral. Aurora forgot to ask youth for her lover, and though Tithonus is immortal, he is old. Achilles is not quite invulnerable; the sacred waters did not wash the heel by which Thetis held him. Siegfried, in the Nibelungen, is not quite immortal, for a leaf fell on his back whilst he was bathing in the dragon's blood, and that spot which it covered is mortal. And so it must be. There is a crack in every thing God has made. It would seem, there is always this vindictive circumstance stealing in at unawares, even into the wild poesy in which the human fancy attempted to make bold holiday, and to shake itself free of the old laws,—this back-stroke, this kick of the gun, certifying that the law is fatal; that in nature nothing can be given, all things are sold.

This is that ancient doctrine of Nemesis, who keeps watch in the universe, and lets no offence go unchastised. The Furies, they said, are attendants on justice, and if the sun in heaven should transgress his path, they would punish him. The poets related that stone walls, and iron swords, and leathern thongs had an occult sympathy with the wrongs of their owners; that the belt which Ajax gave Hector dragged the Trojan hero over the field at the wheels of the car of Achilles, and the sword which Hector gave Ajax was that on whose point Ajax fell. They recorded, that when the Thasians erected a statue to Theagenes, a victor in the games, one of his rivals went to it by night, and endeavoured to throw it down by repeated blows, until at last he moved it from its pedestal, and was crushed to death beneath its fall.

This voice of fable has in it somewhat divine. It came from thought above the will of the writer. That is the best part of each writer, which has nothing private in it; that which he does not know; that which flowed out of his constitution, and not from his too active invention; that which in the study of a single artist you might not easily find, but in the study of many, you would abstract as the spirit of them all. Phidias it is not, but the work of man in that early Hellenic world, that I would know. The name and circumstance of Phidias, however convenient for history, embarrass when we come to the highest criticism. We are to see that which man was tending to do in a given period, and was hindered, or, if you will, modified in doing, by the interfering volitions of Phidias, of Dante, of Shakspeare, the organ whereby man at the moment wrought.

Still more striking is the expression of this fact in the proverbs of all nations, which are always the literature of reason, or the statements of an absolute truth, without qualification. Proverbs, like the sacred books of each nation, are the sanctuary of the intuitions. That which the

droning world, chained to appearances, will not allow
the realist to say in his own words, it will suffer him to
say in proverbs without contradiction. And this law of
laws which the pulpit, the senate, and the college deny,
is hourly preached in all markets and workshops by
flights of proverbs, whose teaching is as true and as
omnipresent as that of birds and flies.

All things are double, one against another.—Tit for
tat; an eye for an eye; a tooth for a tooth; blood for
blood; measure for measure; love for love.—Give and it
shall be given you.—He that watereth shall be watered
himself.—What will you have? quoth God; pay for it and
take it.—Nothing venture, nothing have.—Thou shalt be
paid exactly for what thou hast done, no more, no less.—
Who doth not work shall not eat.—Harm watch, harm
catch.—Curses always recoil on the head of him who
imprecates them.—If you put a chain around the neck of
a slave, the other end fastens itself around your own.—
Bad counsel confounds the adviser.—The Devil is an ass.

It is thus written, because it is thus in life. Our action
is overmastered and characterized above our will by the
law of nature. We aim at a petty end quite aside from the
public good, but our act arranges itself by irresistible
magnetism in a line with the poles of the world.

A man cannot speak but he judges himself. With his
will, or against his will, he draws his portrait to the eye
of his companions by every word. Every opinion reacts
on him who utters it. It is a thread-ball thrown at a mark,
but the other end remains in the thrower's bag. Or,
rather, it is a harpoon hurled at the whale, unwinding, as
it flies, a coil of cord in the boat, and if the harpoon is
not good, or not well thrown, it will go nigh to cut the
steersman in twain, or to sink the boat.

You cannot do wrong without suffering wrong. "No

man had ever a point of pride that was not injurious to him," said Burke. The exclusive in fashionable life does not see that he excludes himself from enjoyment, in the attempt to appropriate it. The exclusionist in religion does not see that he shuts the door of heaven on himself, in striving to shut out others. Treat men as pawns and ninepins, and you shall suffer as well as they. If you leave out their heart, you shall lose your own. The senses would make things of all persons; of women, of children, of the poor. The vulgar proverb, "I will get it from his purse or get it from his skin," is sound philosophy.

All infractions of love and equity in our social relations are speedily punished. They are punished by fear. Whilst I stand in simple relations to my fellow-man, I have no displeasure in meeting him. We meet as water meets water, or as two currents of air mix, with perfect diffusion and interpenetration of nature. But as soon as there is any departure from simplicity, and attempt at half-ness, or good for me that is not good for him, my neighbour feels the wrong; he shrinks from me as far as I have shrunk from him; his eyes no longer seek mine; there is war between us; there is hate in him and fear in me.

All the old abuses in society, universal and particular, all unjust accumulations of property and power, are avenged in the same manner. Fear is an instructer of great sagacity, and the herald of all revolutions. One thing he teaches, that there is rottenness where he appears. He is a carrion crow, and though you see not well what he hovers for, there is death somewhere. Our property is timid, our laws are timid, our cultivated classes are timid. Fear for ages has boded and mowed and gibbered over government and property. That obscene bird is not there for nothing. He indicates great wrongs which must be revised.

Of the like nature is that expectation of change which instantly follows the suspension of our voluntary activity. The terror of cloudless noon, the emerald of Polycrates, the awe of prosperity, the instinct which leads every generous soul to impose on itself tasks of a noble asceticism and vicarious virtue, are the tremblings of the balance of justice through the heart and mind of man.

Experienced men of the world know very well that it is best to pay scot and lot as they go along, and that a man often pays dear for a small frugality. The borrower runs in his own debt. Has a man gained any thing who has received a hundred favors and rendered none? Has he gained by borrowing, through indolence or cunning, his neighbour's wares, or horses, or money? There arises on the deed the instant acknowledgment of benefit on the one part, and of debt on the other; that is, of superiority and inferiority. The transaction remains in the memory of himself and his neighbour; and every new transaction alters, according to its nature, their relation to each other. He may soon come to see that he had better have broken his own bones than to have ridden in his neighbour's coach, and that "the highest price he can pay for a thing is to ask for it."

A wise man will extend this lesson to all parts of life, and know that it is the part of prudence to face every claimant, and pay every just demand on your time, your talents, or your heart. Always pay; for, first or last, you must pay your entire debt. Persons and events may stand for a time between you and justice, but it is only a postponement. You must pay at last your own debt. If you are wise, you will dread a prosperity which only loads you with more. Benefit is the end of nature. But for every benefit which you receive, a tax is levied. He is great who confers the most benefits. He is base—and that is the one base thing in the universe—to receive favors and render none. In the order of nature we cannot render benefits to those from whom we receive them, or only seldom. But the benefit we receive must be rendered again, line for line, deed for deed, cent for cent, to somebody. Beware of too much good staying in your hand. It will fast corrupt and worm worms. Pay it away quickly in some sort.

Labor is watched over by the same pitiless laws. Cheapest, say the prudent, is the dearest labor. What we buy in a broom, a mat, a wagon, a knife, is some application of good sense to a common want. It is best to pay in your land a skilful gardener, or to buy good sense applied to gardening; in your sailor, good sense applied to navigation; in the house, good sense applied to cooking, sewing, serving; in your agent, good sense applied to accounts and affairs. So do you multiply your presence, or spread yourself throughout your estate. But because of the dual constitution of things, in labor as in life there can be no cheating. The thief steals from himself. The swindler swindles himself. For the real price of labor is knowledge and virtue, whereof wealth and credit are signs. These signs, like paper money, may be counterfeited or stolen, but that which they represent, namely, knowledge and virtue, cannot be counterfeited or stolen. These ends of labor cannot be answered but by real exertions of the mind, and in obedience to pure motives. The cheat, the defaulter, the gambler, cannot extort the knowledge of material and moral nature which his honest care and pains yield to the operative. The law of nature is, Do the thing, and you shall have the power: but they who do not the thing have not the power.

Human labor, through all its forms, from the sharpening of a stake to the construction of a city or an epic, is one immense illustration of the perfect compensation of the universe. The absolute balance of Give and Take, the doctrine that every thing has its price,—and if that price is not paid, not that thing but something else is obtained, and that it is impossible to get any thing without its price,—is not less sublime in the columns of a leger than in the budgets of states, in the laws of light and darkness, in all the action and reaction of nature. I cannot doubt that the high laws which each man sees implicated in those processes with which he is conversant, the stern ethics which sparkle on his chisel-edge, which are measured out by his plumb and foot-rule, which stand as manifest in the footing of the shop-bill as in the history of a state,—do recommend to him his trade, and though seldom named, exalt his business to his imagination.

The league between virtue and nature engages all things to assume a hostile front to vice. The beautiful laws and substances of the world persecute and whip the traitor. He finds that things are arranged for truth and benefit, but there is no den in the wide world to hide a rogue. Commit a crime, and the earth is made of glass. Commit a crime, and it seems as if a coat of snow fell on the ground, such as reveals in the woods the track of every partridge and fox and squirrel and mole. You cannot recall the spoken word, you cannot wipe out the foot-track, you cannot draw up the ladder, so as to leave no inlet or clew. Some damning circumstance always transpires. The laws and substances of nature—water, snow, wind, gravitation—become penalties to the thief.

On the other hand, the law holds with equal sureness for all right action. Love, and you shall be loved. All love is mathematically just, as much as the two sides of an algebraic equation. The good man has absolute good,

which like fire turns every thing to its own nature, so that
you cannot do him any harm; but as the royal armies
sent against Napoleon, when he approached, cast down
their colors and from enemies became friends, so disas-
ters of all kinds, as sickness, offence, poverty, prove
benefactors:—

> "Winds blow and waters roll
> Strength to the brave, and power and deity,
> Yet in themselves are nothing."

The good are befriended even by weakness and
defect. As no man had ever a point of pride that was not
injurious to him, so no man had ever a defect that was
not somewhere made useful to him. The stag in the fable
admired his horns and blamed his feet, but when the
hunter came, his feet saved him, and afterwards, caught
in the thicket, his horns destroyed him. Every man in his
lifetime needs to thank his faults. As no man thoroughly
understands a truth until he has contended against it, so
no man has a thorough acquaintance with the hindrances
or talents of men, until he has suffered from the one, and
seen the triumph of the other over his own want of the
same. Has he a defect of temper that unfits him to live in
society? Thereby he is driven to entertain himself alone,
and acquire habits of self-help; and thus, like the wound-
ed oyster, he mends his shell with pearl.

Our strength grows out of our weakness. The indignation which arms itself with secret forces does not
awaken until we are pricked and stung and sorely
assailed. A great man is always willing to be little. Whilst
he sits on the cushion of advantages, he goes to sleep.
When he is pushed, tormented, defeated, he has a
chance to learn something; he has been put on his wits,
on his manhood; he has gained facts; learns his igno-

rance; is cured of the insanity of conceit; has got moderation and real skill. The wise man throws himself on the side of his assailants. It is more his interest than it is theirs to find his weak point. The wound cicatrizes and falls off from him like a dead skin, and when they would triumph, lo! he has passed on invulnerable. Blame is safer than praise. I hate to be defended in a newspaper. As long as all that is said is said against me, I feel a certain assurance of success. But as soon as honeyed words of praise are spoken for me, I feel as one that lies unprotected before his enemies. In general, every evil to which we do not succumb is a benefactor. As the Sandwich Islander believes that the strength and valor of the enemy he kills passes into himself, so we gain the strength of the temptation we resist.

The same guards which protect us from disaster, defect, and enmity, defend us, if we will, from selfishness and fraud. Bolts and bars are not the best of our institutions, nor is shrewdness in trade a mark of wisdom. Men suffer all their life long, under the foolish superstition that they can be cheated. But it is as impossible for a man to be cheated by any one but himself, as for a thing to be and not to be at the same time. There is a third silent party to all our bargains. The nature and soul of things takes on itself the guaranty of the fulfilment of every contract, so that honest service cannot come to loss. If you serve an ungrateful master, serve him the more. Put God in your debt. Every stroke shall be repaid. The longer the payment is withholden, the better for you; for compound interest on compound interest is the rate and usage of this exchequer.

The history of persecution is a history of endeavours to cheat nature, to make water run up hill, to twist a rope of sand. It makes no difference whether the actors be many or one, a tyrant or a mob. A mob is a society of bodies voluntarily bereaving themselves of reason, and traversing its work. The mob is man voluntarily descending to the nature of the beast. Its fit hour of activity is night. Its actions are insane like its whole constitution. It persecutes a principle; it would whip a right; it would tar and feather justice, by inflicting fire and outrage upon the houses and persons of those who have these. It resembles the prank of boys, who run with fire-engines to put out the ruddy aurora streaming to the stars. The inviolate spirit turns their spite against the wrongdoers. The martyr cannot be dishonored. Every lash inflicted is a tongue of fame; every prison, a more illustrious abode; every burned book or house enlightens the world; every suppressed or expunged word reverberates through the earth from side to side. Hours of sanity and consideration are always arriving to communities, as to individuals, when the truth is seen, and the martyrs are justified.

Thus do all things preach the indifferency of circumstances. The man is all. Every thing has two sides, a good and an evil. Every advantage has its tax. I learn to be content. But the doctrine of compensation is not the doctrine of indifferency. The thoughtless say, on hearing these representations,—What boots it to do well? there is one event to good and evil; if I gain any good, I must pay for it; if I lose any good, I gain some other; all actions are indifferent.

There is a deeper fact in the soul than compensation, to wit, its own nature. The soul is not a compensation, but a life. The soul *is*. Under all this running sea of circumstance, whose waters ebb and flow with perfect balance, lies the aboriginal abyss of real Being. Essence, or God, is not a relation, or a part, but the whole. Being is the vast affirmative, excluding negation, self-balanced, and swallowing up all relations, parts, and times within itself. Nature, truth, virtue, are the influx from thence. Vice is the absence or departure of the same. Nothing, Falsehood, may indeed stand as the great Night or shade, on which, as a background, the living universe paints itself forth; but no fact is begotten by it; it cannot work; for it is not. It cannot work any good; it cannot work any harm. It is harm inasmuch as it is worse not to be than to be.

We feel defrauded of the retribution due to evil acts, because the criminal adheres to his vice and contumacy, and does not come to a crisis or judgment anywhere in visible nature. There is no stunning confutation of his nonsense before men and angels. Has he therefore out-witted the law? Inasmuch as he carries the malignity and the lie with him, he so far deceases from nature. In some manner there will be a demonstration of the wrong to the understanding also; but should we not see it, this deadly deduction makes square the eternal account.

Neither can it be said, on the other hand, that the gain of rectitude must be bought by any loss. There is no penalty to virtue; no penalty to wisdom; they are proper additions of being. In a virtuous action, I properly *am*; in a virtuous act, I add to the world; I plant into deserts conquered from Chaos and Nothing, and see the dark-ness receding on the limits of the horizon. There can be no excess to love; none to knowledge; none to beauty, when these attributes are considered in the purest sense. The soul refuses limits, and always affirms an Optimism, never a Pessimism.

His life is a progress, and not a station. His instinct is trust. Our instinct uses "more" and "less" in application to man, of the *presence of the soul*, and not of its absence;

the brave man is greater than the coward; the true, the benevolent, the wise, is more a man, and not less, than the fool and knave. There is no tax on the good of virtue; for that is the incoming of God himself, or absolute existence, without any comparative. Material good has its tax, and if it came without desert or sweat, has no root in me, and the next wind will blow it away. But all the good of nature is the soul's, and may be had, if paid for in nature's lawful coin, that is, by labor which the heart and the head allow. I no longer wish to meet a good I do not earn, for example, to find a pot of buried gold, knowing that it brings with it new burdens. I do not wish more external goods,—neither possessions, nor honors, nor powers, nor persons. The gain is apparent; the tax is certain. But there is no tax on the knowledge that the compensation exists, and that it is not desirable to dig up treasure. Herein I rejoice with a serene eternal peace. I contract the boundaries of possible mischief. I learn the wisdom of St. Bernard,—"Nothing can work me damage except myself; the harm that I sustain I carry about with me, and never am a real sufferer but by my own fault."

In the nature of the soul is the compensation for the inequalities of condition. The radical tragedy of nature seems to be the distinction of More and Less. How can Less not feel the pain; how not feel indignation or malevolence towards More? Look at those who have less faculty, and one feels sad, and knows not well what to make of it. He almost shuns their eye; he fears they will upbraid God. What should they do? It seems a great injustice. But see the facts nearly, and these mountainous inequalities vanish. Love reduces them, as the sun melts the iceberg in the sea. The heart and soul of all men being one, this bitterness of *His* and *Mine* ceases. His is mine. I am my brother, and my brother is me. If I feel overshadowed and outdone by great neighbours, I can yet love; I can still receive; and he that loveth maketh his own the grandeur he loves. Thereby I make the discovery that my brother is my guardian, acting for me with the friendliest designs, and the estate I so admired and envied is my own. It is the nature of the soul to appropriate all things. Jesus and Shakspeare are fragments of the soul, and by love I conquer and incorporate them in my own conscious domain. His virtue,—is not that mine? His wit,—if it cannot be made mine, it is not wit.

Such, also, is the natural history of calamity. The changes which break up at short intervals the prosperity of men are advertisements of a nature whose law is growth. Every soul is by this intrinsic necessity quitting its whole system of things, its friends, and home, and laws, and faith, as the shell-fish crawls out of its beautiful but stony case, because it no longer admits of its growth, and slowly forms a new house. In proportion to the vigor of the individual, these revolutions are frequent, until in some happier mind they are incessant, and all worldly relations hang very loosely about him, becoming, as it were, a transparent fluid membrane through which the living form is seen, and not, as in most men, an indurated heterogeneous fabric of many dates, and of no settled character, in which the man is imprisoned. Then there can be enlargement, and the man of to-day scarcely recognizes the man of yesterday. And such should be the outward biography of man in time, a putting off of dead circumstances day by day, as he renews his raiment day by day. But to us, in our lapsed estate, resting, not advancing, resisting, not cooperating with the divine expansion, this growth comes by shocks.

We cannot part with our friends. We cannot let our angels go. We do not see that they only go out, that archangels may come in. We are idolaters of the old. We do not believe in the riches of the soul, in its proper eternity and omnipresence. We do not believe there is any force in to-day to rival or recreate that beautiful yesterday. We linger in the ruins of the old tent, where once we had bread and shelter and organs, nor believe that the spirit can feed, cover, and nerve us again. We cannot again find aught so dear, so sweet, so graceful. But we sit and weep in vain. The voice of the Almighty saith, 'Up and onward for evermore!' We cannot stay amid the ruins. Neither will we rely on the new; and so we walk ever with reverted eyes, like those monsters who look backwards.

And yet the compensations of calamity are made apparent to the understanding also, after long intervals of time. A fever, a mutilation, a cruel disappointment, a loss of wealth, a loss of friends, seems at the moment unpaid loss, and unpayable. But the sure years reveal the deep remedial force that underlies all facts. The death of a dear friend, wife, brother, lover, which seemed nothing but privation, somewhat later assumes the aspect of a guide or genius; for it commonly operates revolutions in our way of life, terminates an epoch of infancy or of youth which was waiting to be closed, breaks up a wonted occupation, or a household, or style of living, and allows the formation of new ones more friendly to the growth of character. It permits or constrains the formation of new acquaintances, and the reception of new influences that prove of the first importance to the next years; and the man or woman who would have remained a sunny garden-flower, with no room for its roots and too much sunshine for its head, by the falling of the walls and the neglect of the gardener, is made the banian of the forest, yielding shade and fruit to wide neighbourhoods of men.

The Essay
"Spiritual Laws"

"Spiritual Laws" reveals Emerson at his most accessible, both intellectually and emotionally. It is as if he were the most comfortable speaking of spiritual laws and in that relaxed confidence allowed us to know him well. In this essay his essential compassion for others emerges as helpful guidance in the practical problems of living: how to recognize and use our talents; how to know what we should be doing.

Emerson knew, for example, what his talents were and how he must use them. His was a talent for speaking and writing on the higher questions of existence and for leading a contemplative life. When asked to participate in the burning political and social questions of his day, he did so with great reluctance. At the beginning of his essay "The Fugitive Slave Law," he expressed that reluctance and at the same time directed our attention to the real focus of his life's work:

I do not often speak to public questions;—they are odious and hurtful, and it seems like meddling or leaving your work. I have my own spirits in prison;—spirits in deeper prisons, whom no man visits if I do not. And then I see what havoc it makes with any good mind, a dissipated philanthropy. The

> one thing not to be forgiven to intellectual persons
> is, not to know their own task. . . .

The centerpiece of Greek philosophy is the oracular admonition Know Thyself. To the Classical Greeks the admonition might have meant Know Your Limits, your place in the scheme of things. Know Necessity, that powerful force that binds us all to existence and mortality. At a higher level of perception, however, where Plato and the Hellenistic thinkers dwelled, Know Thyself revealed that point in the mind where the philosopher engaged the fundamental questions of his existence. Know Thyself means Know Who You Are as well as Know Your Task. Ideally, knowing who we are and what our task is allows us, as Emerson puts it, to sweep "serenely over a deepening channel into an infinite sea."

Central to his guidance in this essay is the admonition *Do not choose.* Instead we are to watch, wait, and respond when we have been called. In "The Transcendentalist" Emerson addressed the criticism heaped upon the followers of Idealism that they did nothing; they were not useful to the culture. The materialist was a man of action, a doer. There was, after all, a wilderness to be conquered in 1840. Emerson's reflective stance identified another force to which we owed our obedience. Talent was the call, how the Universal Order had organized itself in our being.

The rhetoric of this essay reverses ordinary ideation. We are shocked into turning around and seeing in another way, like bending over and looking at the landscape from between our legs.

> By doing his work he makes the need felt which he
> can supply, and creates the taste by which he is
> enjoyed. By doing his own work he unfolds himself.

Emerson's method is exposed here dramatically. Normally, we look around for some need to arise and then we go about filling it, and we wait to see what the public taste demands before we begin to create. The result of such perversion is decadence and the numbing labor that has nothing to do with the unfolding self. Integrity requires that we find our talents and then direct our attention to developing what that talent demands of us. Being fully human, insofar as we embody partially the human archetype, means finding a fitting expression for the talent we have been given. If the soul had need of an organ here, as Emerson said, who am I to ignore its calling?

The best way to read Emerson is to suppose that what he says is indeed true and then to experiment with his guidance. It is a healthful diet and will soon get us into shape. There is a helpful trick in matters of following guidance. It goes like this: Suppose for a moment that recommended steps might in fact be helpful and proceed *as if* the advice were true for you. After a while, when the results begin to appear satisfying, when actual experience is positive, we then let go of the *as if* part of the equation and begin to adopt the guidance as a way of life. Soon, we begin to speak from experience in these matters and begin to "measure the accumulations of the subtle element." Without our knowing it or willing it, our lives have changed.

SPIRITUAL LAWS

The living Heaven thy prayers respect,
House at once and architect,
Quarrying man's rejected hours,
Builds therewith eternal towers;

Sole and self-commanded works,
Fears not undermining days,
Grows by decays,
And, by the famous might that lurks
In reaction and recoil,
Makes flame to freeze, and ice to boil;
Forging, through swart arms of Offence,
The silver seat of Innocence.

When the act of reflection takes place in the mind, when we look at ourselves in the light of thought, we discover that our life is embosomed in beauty. Behind us, as we go, all things assume pleasing forms, as clouds do far off. Not only things familiar and stale, but even the tragic and terrible, are comely, as they take their place in the pictures of memory. The river-bank, the weed at the water-side, the old house, the foolish person,—however neglected in the passing,—have a grace in the past. Even the corpse that has lain in the chambers has added a solemn ornament to the house. The soul will not know either deformity or pain. If, in the hours of clear reason, we should speak the severest truth, we should say, that we had never made a sacrifice. In these hours the mind seems so great, that nothing can be taken from us that seems much. All loss, all pain, is particular; the universe remains to the heart unhurt. Neither vexations nor calamities abate our trust. No man ever stated his griefs as lightly as he might. Allow for exaggeration in the most patient and sorely ridden hack that ever was driven. For it is only the finite that has wrought and suffered; the infinite lies stretched in smiling repose.

The intellectual life may be kept clean and healthful, if man will live the life of nature, and not import into his mind difficulties which are none of his. No man need be perplexed in his speculations. Let him do and say what strictly belongs to him, and, though very ignorant of books, his nature shall not yield him any intellectual obstructions and doubts. Our young people are diseased with the theological problems of original sin, origin of evil, predestination, and the like. These never presented a practical difficulty to any man,—never darkened across any man's road, who did not go out of his way to seek them. These are the soul's mumps, and measles, and whooping-coughs, and those who have not caught them cannot describe their health or prescribe the cure. A simple mind will not know these enemies. It is quite another thing that he should be able to give account of his faith, and expound to another the theory of his self-union and freedom. This requires rare gifts. Yet, without this self-knowledge, there may be a sylvan strength and integrity in that which he is. "A few strong instincts and a few plain rules" suffice us.

My will never gave the images in my mind the rank they now take. The regular course of studies, the years of academical and professional education, have not yielded me better facts than some idle books under the bench at the Latin School. What we do not call education is more precious than that which we call so. We form no guess, at the time of receiving a thought, of its comparative value. And education often wastes its effort in attempts to thwart and balk this natural magnetism, which is sure to select what belongs to it.

In like manner, our moral nature is vitiated by any interference of our will. People represent virtue as a struggle, and take to themselves great airs upon their attainments, and the question is everywhere vexed, when a noble nature is commended, whether the man is not better who strives with temptation. But there is no merit in the matter. Either God is there, or he is not there. We love characters in proportion as they are impulsive and spontaneous. The less a man thinks or knows about his virtues, the better we like him. Timoleon's victories are the best victories; which ran and flowed like Homer's verses, Plutarch said. When we see a soul whose acts are all regal, graceful, and pleasant as roses, we must thank God that such things can be and are, and not turn sourly on the angel, and say, 'Crump is a better man with his grunting resistance to all his native devils.'

Not less conspicuous is the preponderance of nature over will in all practical life. There is less intention in history than we ascribe to it. We impute deep-laid, far-sighted plans to Caesar and Napoleon; but the best of their power was in nature, not in them. Men of an extra-ordinary success, in their honest moments, have always sung, 'Not unto us, not unto us.' According to the faith of their times, they have built altars to Fortune, or to Destiny, or to St. Julian. Their success lay in their parallel-ism to the course of thought, which found in them an unobstructed channel; and the wonders of which they were the visible conductors seemed to the eye their deed. Did the wires generate the galvanism? It is even true that there was less in them on which they could reflect, than in an other; as the virtue of a pipe is to be smooth and hollow. That which externally seemed will and immovableness was willingness and self-annihila-tion. Could Shakspeare give a theory of Shakspeare? Could ever a man of prodigious mathematical genius convey to others any insight into his methods? If he could communicate that secret, it would instantly lose its exaggerated value, blending with the daylight and the vital energy the power to stand and to go.

The lesson is forcibly taught by these observations,

THE ESSAY "SPIRITUAL LAWS"

that our life might be much easier and simpler than we make it; that the world might be a happier place than it is; that there is no need of struggles, convulsions, and despairs, of the wringing of the hands and the gnashing of the teeth; that we miscreate our own evils. We interfere with the optimism of nature; for, whenever we get this vantage-ground of the past, or of a wiser mind in the present, we are able to discern that we are begirt with laws which execute themselves.

The face of external nature teaches the same lesson. Nature will not have us fret and fume. She does not like our benevolence or our learning much better than she likes our frauds and wars. When we come out of the caucus, or the bank, or the Abolition-convention, or the Temperance-meeting, or the Transcendental club, into the fields and woods, she says to us, 'So hot? my little Sir.'

We are full of mechanical actions. We must needs intermeddle, and have things in our own way, until the sacrifices and virtues of society are odious. Love should make joy; but our benevolence is unhappy. Our Sunday-schools, and churches, and pauper-societies are yokes to the neck. We pain ourselves to please nobody. There are natural ways of arriving at the same ends at which these aim, but do not arrive. Why should all virtue work in one and the same way? Why should all give dollars? It is very inconvenient to us country folk, and we do not think any good will come of it. We have not dollars; merchants have; let them give them. Farmers will give corn; poets will sing; women will sew; laborers will lend a hand; the children will bring flowers. And why drag this dead weight of a Sunday-school over the whole Christendom? It is natural and beautiful that childhood should inquire, and maturity should teach; but it is time enough to answer questions when they are asked. Do not shut up the young people against their will in a pew, and force the children to ask them questions for an hour against their will.

If we look wider, things are all alike; laws, and letters, and creeds, and modes of living, seem a travestie of truth. Our society is encumbered by ponderous machinery, which resembles the endless aqueducts which the Romans built over hill and dale, and which are superseded by the discovery of the law that water rises to the level of its source. It is a Chinese wall which any nimble Tartar can leap over. It is a standing army, not so good as a peace. It is a graduated, titled, richly appointed empire, quite superfluous when town-meetings are found to answer just as well.

Let us draw a lesson from nature, which always works by short ways. When the fruit is ripe, it falls. When the fruit is despatched, the leaf falls. The circuit of the waters is mere falling. The walking of man and all animals is a falling forward. All our manual labor and works of strength, as prying, splitting, digging, rowing, and so forth, are done by dint of continual falling, and the globe, earth, moon, comet, sun, star, fall for ever and ever.

The simplicity of the universe is very different from the simplicity of a machine. He who sees moral nature out and out, and thoroughly knows how knowledge is acquired and character formed, is a pedant. The simplicity of nature is not that which may easily be read, but is inexhaustible. The last analysis can no wise be made. We judge of a man's wisdom by his hope, knowing that the perception of the inexhaustibleness of nature is an immortal youth. The wild fertility of nature is felt in comparing our rigid names and reputations with our fluid consciousness. We pass in the world for sects and schools, for erudition and piety, and we are all the time jejune babes. One sees very well how Pyrrhonism grew up. Every man sees that he is that middle point, whereof every thing may be affirmed and denied with equal reason. He is old, he is young, he is very wise, he is altogether ignorant. He hears and feels what you say of the seraphim, and of the tin-peddler. There is no permanent wise man, except in the figment of the Stoics. We side with the hero, as we read or paint, against the coward and the robber; but we have been ourselves that coward and robber, and shall be again, not in the low circumstance, but in comparison with the grandeurs possible to the soul.

A little consideration of what takes place around us every day would show us, that a higher law than that of our will regulates events; that our painful labors are unnecessary, and fruitless; that only in our easy, simple, spontaneous action are we strong, and by contenting ourselves with obedience we become divine. Belief and love,—a believing love will relieve us of a vast load of care. O my brothers, God exists. There is a soul at the centre of nature, and over the will of every man, so that none of us can wrong the universe. It has so infused its strong enchantment into nature, that we prosper when we accept its advice, and when we struggle to wound its creatures, our hands are glued to our sides, or they beat our own breasts. The whole course of things goes to teach us faith. We need only obey. There is guidance for each of us, and by lowly listening we shall hear the right word. Why need you choose so painfully your place, and occupation, and associates, and modes of action, and of entertainment? Certainly there is a possible right for you that precludes the need of balance and wilful election.

For you there is a reality, a fit place and congenial duties. Place yourself in the middle of the stream of power and wisdom which animates all whom it floats, and you are without effort impelled to truth, to right, and a perfect contentment. Then you put all gainsayers in the wrong. Then you are the world, the measure of right, of truth, of beauty. If we will not be mar-plots with our miserable interferences, the work, the society, letters, arts, science, religion of men would go on far better than now, and the heaven predicted from the beginning of the world, and still predicted from the bottom of the heart, would organize itself, as do now the rose, and the air, and the sun.

I say, *do not choose*; but that is a figure of speech by which I would distinguish what is commonly called *choice* among men, and which is a partial act, the choice of the hands, of the eyes, of the appetites, and not a whole act of the man. But that which I call right or goodness is the choice of my constitution; and that which I call heaven, and inwardly aspire after, is the state or circumstance desirable to my constitution; and the action which I in all my years tend to do, is the work for my faculties. We must hold a man amenable to reason for the choice of his daily craft or profession. It is not an excuse any longer for his deeds, that they are the custom of his trade. What business has he with an evil trade? Has he not a *calling* in his character.

Each man has his own vocation. The talent is the call. There is one direction in which all space is open to him. He has faculties silently inviting him thither to endless exertion. He is like a ship in a river; he runs against obstructions on every side but one; on that side all obstruction is taken away, and he sweeps serenely over a deepening channel into an infinite sea. This talent and this call depend on his organization, or the mode in which the general soul incarnates itself in him. He inclines to do something which is easy to him, and good when it is done, but which no other man can do. He has no rival. For the more truly he consults his own powers, the more difference will his work exhibit from the work of any other. His ambition is exactly proportioned to his powers. The height of the pinnacle is determined by the breadth of the base. Every man has this call of the power to do somewhat unique, and no man has any other call. The pretence that he has another call, a summons by name and personal election and outward "signs that mark him extraordinary, and not in the roll of common men," is fanaticism, and betrays obtuseness to perceive that there is one mind in all the individuals, and no respect of persons therein.

By doing his work, he makes the need felt which he can supply, and creates the taste by which he is enjoyed. By doing his own work, he unfolds himself. It is the vice of our public speaking that it has not abandonment. Somewhere, not only every orator but every man should let out all the length of all the reins; should find or make a frank and hearty expression of what force and meaning is in him. The common experience is, that the man fits himself as well as he can to the customary details of that work or trade he falls into, and tends it as a dog turns a spit. Then is he a part of the machine he moves; the man is lost. Until he can manage to communicate himself to others in his full stature and proportion, he does not yet find his vocation. He must find in that an outlet for his character, so that he may justify his work to their eyes. If the labor is mean, let him by his thinking and character make it liberal. Whatever he knows and thinks, whatever in his apprehension is worth doing, that let him communicate, or men will never know and honor him aright.

Foolish, whenever you take the meanness and formality of that thing you do, instead of converting it into the obedient spiracle of your character and aims.

We like only such actions as have already long had the praise of men, and do not perceive that any thing man can do may be divinely done. We think greatness entailed or organized in some places or duties, in certain offices or occasions, and do not see that Paganini can extract rapture from a catgut, and Eulenstein from a jews-harp, and a nimble-fingered lad out of shreds of paper with his scissors, and Landseer out of swine, and the hero out of the pitiful habitation and company in which he was hidden. What we call obscure condition or vulgar society is that condition and society whose poetry is not yet written, but which you shall presently make as enviable and renowned as any. In our estimates, let us take a lesson from kings. The parts of hospitality, the connection of families, the impressiveness of death, and a thousand other things, royalty makes its own estimate of, and a royal mind will. To make habitually a new estimate,— that is elevation.

What a man does, that he has. What has he to do with hope or fear? In himself is his might. Let him regard no good as solid, but that which is in his nature, and which must grow out of him as long as he exists. The goods of fortune may come and go like summer leaves; let him scatter them on every wind as the momentary signs of his infinite productiveness.

He may have his own. A man's genius, the quality that differences him from every other, the susceptibility to one class of influences, the selection of what is fit for him, the rejection of what is unfit, determines for him the character of the universe. A man is a method, a progressive arrangement; a selecting principle, gathering his like to him, wherever he goes. He takes only his own out of the multiplicity that sweeps and circles round him. He is like one of those booms which are set out from the shore on rivers to catch drift-wood, or like the loadstone amongst splinters of steel. Those facts, words, persons, which dwell in his memory without his being able to say why, remain, because they have a relation to him not less real for being as yet unapprehended. They are symbols of value to him, as they can interpret parts of his consciousness which he would vainly seek words for in the conventional images of books and other minds. What attracts my attention shall have it, as I will go to the man who knocks at my door, whilst a thousand persons, as worthy, go by it, to whom I give no regard. It is enough that these particulars speak to me. A few anecdotes, a few traits of character, manners, face, a few incidents, have an emphasis in your memory out of all proportion to their apparent significance, if you measure them by the ordinary standards. They relate to your gift. Let them have their weight, and do not reject them, and cast about for illustration and facts more usual in literature. What your heart thinks great is great. The soul's emphasis is always right.

Over all things that are agreeable to his nature and genius, the man has the highest right. Everywhere he may take what belongs to his spiritual estate, nor can he take any thing else, though all doors were open, nor can all the force of men hinder him from taking so much. It is vain to attempt to keep a secret from one who has a right to know it. It will tell itself. That mood into which a friend can bring us is his dominion over us. To the thoughts of that state of mind he has a right. All the secrets of that state of mind he can compel. This is a law which statesmen use in practice. All the terrors of the French Republic, which held Austria in awe, were unable to command her diplomacy. But Napoleon sent to Vienna M. de Narbonne, one of the old noblesse, with the morals, manners, and name of that interest, saying, that it was indispensable to send to the old aristocracy of Europe men of the same connection, which, in fact, constitutes a sort of free-masonry. M. de Narbonne, in less than a fortnight, penetrated all the secrets of the imperial cabinet.

Nothing seems so easy as to speak and to be understood. Yet a man may come to find *that* the strongest of defences and of ties,—that he has been understood; and he who has received an opinion may come to find it the most inconvenient of bonds.

If a teacher have any opinion which he wishes to conceal, his pupils will become as fully indoctrinated into that as into any which he publishes. If you pour water into a vessel twisted into coils and angles, it is vain to say, I will pour it only into this or that;—it will find its level in all. Men feel and act the consequences of your doctrine, without being able to show how they follow. Show us an arc of the curve, and a good mathematician will find out the whole figure. We are always reasoning from the seen to the unseen. Hence the perfect intelligence that subsists between wise men of remote ages. A man cannot bury his meanings so deep in his book, but time and like-minded men will find them. Plato had a secret doctrine, had he? What secret can he conceal from the eyes of Bacon? of Montaigne? of Kant? Therefore, Aristotle said of his works, "They are published and not published."

No man can learn what he has not preparation for learning, however near to his eyes is the object. A chemist may tell his most precious secrets to a carpenter, and he shall be never the wiser,—the secrets he would not utter to a chemist for an estate. God screens us evermore from premature ideas. Our eyes are holden that we cannot see things that stare us in the face, until the hour arrives when the mind is ripened; then we behold them, and the time when we saw them not is like a dream.

Not in nature but in man is all the beauty and worth he sees. The world is very empty, and is indebted to this gilding, exalting soul for all its pride. "Earth fills her lap with splendors" *not her own.* The vale of Tempe, Tivoli, and Rome are earth and water, rocks and sky. There are as good earth and water in a thousand places, yet how unaffecting!

People are not the better for the sun and moon, the horizon and the trees; as it is not observed that the keepers of Roman galleries, or the valets of painters, have any elevation of thought, or that librarians are wiser men than others. There are graces in the demeanour of a polished and noble person, which are lost upon the eye of a churl. These are like the stars whose light has not yet reached us.

He may see what he maketh. Our dreams are the sequel of our waking knowledge. The visions of the night bear some proportion to the visions of the day. Hideous dreams are exaggerations of the sins of the day. We see our evil affections embodied in bad physiognomies. On the Alps, the traveller sometimes beholds his own shadow magnified to a giant, so that every gesture of his hand is terrific. "My children," said an old man to his boys scared by a figure in the dark entry, "my children, you will never see any thing worse than yourselves." As in dreams, so in the scarcely less fluid events of the world, every man sees himself in colossal, without knowing that it is himself. The good, compared to the evil which he sees, is as his own good to his own evil. Every quality of his mind is magnified in some one

acquaintance, and every emotion of his heart in some
one. He is like a quincunx of trees, which counts five,
east, west, north, or south; or, an initial, medial, and ter-
minal acrostic. And why not? He cleaves to one person,
and avoids another, according to their likeness or unlike-
ness to himself, truly seeking himself in his associates,
and moreover in his trade, and habits, and gestures, and
meats, and drinks; and comes at last to be faithfully represented by every view you take of his circumstances.

He may read what he writes. What can we see or
acquire, but what we are? You have observed a skilful
man reading Virgil. Well, that author is a thousand books
to a thousand persons. Take the book into your two
hands, and read your eyes out; you will never find what
I find. If any ingenious reader would have a monopoly
of the wisdom or delight he gets, he is as secure now the
book is Englished, as if it were imprisoned in the Pelews'
tongue. It is with a good book as it is with good company. Introduce a base person among gentlemen; it is all to
no purpose; he is not their fellow. Every society protects
itself. The company is perfectly safe, and he is not one of
them, though his body is in the room.

What avails it to fight with the eternal laws of mind,
which adjust the relation of all persons to each other, by
the mathematical measure of their havings and beings?
Gertrude is enamoured of Guy; how high, how aristocratic, how Roman his mien and manners! to live with
him were life indeed, and no purchase is too great; and
heaven and earth are moved to that end. Well, Gertrude
has Guy; but what now avails how high, how aristocratic,
how Roman his mien and manners, if his heart and aims
are in the senate, in the theatre, and in the billiard-room,
and she has no aims, no conversation, that can enchant
her graceful lord?

He shall have his own society. We can love nothing but nature. The most wonderful talents, the most meritorious exertions, really avail very little with us; but nearness or likeness of nature,—how beautiful is the ease of its victory! Persons approach us famous for their beauty, for their accomplishments, worthy of all wonder for their charms and gifts; they dedicate their whole skill to the hour and the company, with very imperfect result. To be sure, it would be ungrateful in us not to praise them loudly. Then, when all is done, a person of related mind, a brother or sister by nature, comes to us so softly and easily, so nearly and intimately, as if it were the blood in our proper veins, that we feel as if some one was gone, instead of another having come; we are utterly relieved and refreshed; it is a sort of joyful solitude. We foolishly think in our days of sin, that we must court friends by compliance to the customs of society, to its dress, its breeding, and its estimates. But only that soul can be my friend which I encounter on the line of my own march, that soul to which I do not decline, and which does not decline to me, but, native of the same celestial latitude, repeats in its own all my experience. The scholar forgets himself, and apes the customs and costumes of the man of the world, to deserve the smile of beauty, and follows some giddy girl, not yet taught by religious passion to know the noble woman with all that is serene, oracular, and beautiful in her soul. Let him be great, and love shall follow him. Nothing is more deeply punished than the neglect of the affinities by which alone society should be formed, and the insane levity of choosing associates by others' eyes.

He may set his own rate. It is a maxim worthy of all acceptation, that a man may have that allowance he takes. Take the place and attitude which belong to you, and all men acquiesce. The world must be just. It leaves every man, with profound unconcern, to set his own rate. Hero or driveller, it meddles not in the matter. It will certainly accept your own measure of your doing and being, whether you sneak about and deny your own name, or whether you see your work produced to the concave sphere of the heavens, one with the revolution of the stars.

The same reality pervades all teaching. The man may teach by doing, and not otherwise. If he can communicate himself, he can teach, but not by words. He teaches who gives, and he learns who receives. There is no teaching until the pupil is brought into the same state or principle in which you are; a transfusion takes place; he is you, and you are he; then is a teaching; and by no unfriendly chance or bad company can he ever quite lose the benefit. But your propositions run out of one ear as they ran in at the other. We see it advertised that Mr. Grand will deliver an oration on the Fourth of July, and Mr. Hand before the Mechanics' Association, and we do not go thither, because we know that these gentlemen will not communicate their own character and experience to the company. If we had reason to expect such a confidence, we should go through all inconvenience and opposition. The sick would be carried in litters. But a public oration is an escapade, a non-committal, an apology, a gag, and not a communication, not a speech, not a man.

A like Nemesis presides over all intellectual works. We have yet to learn, that the thing uttered in words is not therefore affirmed. It must affirm itself, or no forms of logic or of oath can give it evidence. The sentence must also contain its own apology for being spoken.

The effect of any writing on the public mind is mathematically measurable by its depth of thought. How much water does it draw? If it awaken you to think, if it lift you from your feet with the great voice of eloquence, then the effect is to be wide, slow, permanent, over the minds of men; if the pages instruct you not, they will die like flies in the hour. The way to speak and write what shall not go out of fashion is, to speak and write sincerely. The argument which has not power to reach my own practice, I may well doubt, will fail to reach yours. But take Sidney's maxim:—"Look in thy heart, and write." He that writes to himself writes to an eternal public. That statement only is fit to be made public, which you have come at in attempting to satisfy your own curiosity. The writer who takes his subject from his ear, and not from his heart, should know that he has lost as much as he seems to have gained, and when the empty book has gathered all its praise, and half the people say, 'What poetry! what genius!' it still needs fuel to make fire. That only profits which is profitable. Life alone can impart life; and though we should burst, we can only be valued as we make ourselves valuable. There is no luck in literary reputation. They who make up the final verdict upon every book are not the partial and noisy readers of the hour when it appears; but a court as of angels, a public not to be bribed, not to be entreated, and not to be over-awed, decides upon every man's title to fame. Only those books come down which deserve to last. Gilt edges, vellum, and morocco, and presentation-copies to all the libraries, will not preserve a book in circulation beyond its intrinsic date. It must go with all Walpole's Noble and Royal Authors to its fate. Blackmore, Kotzebue, or Pollok may endure for a night, but Moses and Homer stand for ever. There are not in the world at any one time more than a dozen persons who read and understand Plato:— never enough to pay for an edition of his works; yet to every generation these come duly down, for the sake of those few persons, as if God brought them in his hand. "No book," said Bentley, "was ever written down by any but itself." The permanence of all books is fixed by no effort friendly or hostile, but by their own specific gravity, or the intrinsic importance of their contents to the constant mind of man. "Do not trouble yourself too much about the light on your statue," said Michel Angelo to the young sculptor; "the light of the public square will test its value."

In like manner the effect of every action is measured by the depth of the sentiment from which it proceeds. The great man knew not that he was great. It took a century or two for that fact to appear. What he did, he did because he must; it was the most natural thing in the world, and grew out of the circumstances of the moment. But now, every thing he did, even to the lifting of his finger or the eating of bread, looks large, all-related, and is called an institution.

These are the demonstrations in a few particulars of the genius of nature; they show the direction of the stream. But the stream is blood; every drop is alive. Truth has not single victories; all things are its organs,—not only dust and stones, but errors and lies. The laws of disease, physicians say, are as beautiful as the laws of health. Our philosophy is affirmative, and readily accepts the testimony of negative facts, as every shadow points to the sun. By a divine necessity, every fact in nature is constrained to offer its testimony.

Human character evermore publishes itself. The most fugitive deed and word, the mere air of doing a thing, the intimated purpose, expresses character. If you act, you show character; if you sit still, if you sleep, you show it. You think, because you have spoken nothing when others spoke, and have given no opinion on the times, on the church, on slavery, on marriage, on socialism, on secret societies, on the college, on parties and persons, that your verdict is still expected with curiosity as a reserved wisdom. Far otherwise; your silence answers very loud. You have no oracle to utter, and your fellow-men have learned that you cannot help them; for, oracles speak. Doth not wisdom cry, and understanding put forth her voice?

Dreadful limits are set in nature to the powers of dissimulation. Truth tyrannizes over the unwilling members of the body. Faces never lie, it is said. No man need be deceived, who will study the changes of expression. When a man speaks the truth in the spirit of truth, his eye is as clear as the heavens. When he has base ends, and speaks falsely, the eye is muddy and sometimes asquint.

I have heard an experienced counsellor say, that he never feared the effect upon a jury of a lawyer who does not believe in his heart that his client ought to have a verdict. If he does not believe it, his unbelief will appear to the jury, despite all his protestations, and will become their unbelief. This is that law whereby a work of art, of whatever kind, sets us in the same state of mind wherein the artist was when he made it. That which we do not believe, we cannot adequately say, though we may repeat the words never so often. It was this conviction which Swedenborg expressed, when he described a group of persons in the spiritual world endeavouring in vain to articulate a proposition which they did not believe; but they could not, though they twisted and folded their lips even to indignation.

A man passes for that he is worth. Very idle is all curiosity concerning other people's estimate of us, and

all fear of remaining unknown is not less so. If a man
know that he can do any thing,—that he can do it better
than any one else,—he has a pledge of the acknowledgment of that fact by all persons. The world is full of judg-
ment-days, and into every assembly that a man enters, in
every action he attempts, he is gauged and stamped. In
every troop of boys that whoop and run in each yard
and square, a new-comer is as well and accurately
weighed in the course of a few days, and stamped with
his right number, as if he had undergone a formal trial of
his strength, speed, and temper. A stranger comes from a
distant school, with better dress, with trinkets in his
pockets, with airs and pretensions: an older boy says to
himself, 'It's of no use; we shall find him out to-morrow.'
'What has he done?' is the divine question which searches men, and transpierces every false reputation. A fop
may sit in any chair of the world, nor be distinguished
for his hour from Homer and Washington; but there need
never be any doubt concerning the respective ability of
human beings. Pretension may sit still, but cannot act.
Pretension never feigned an act of real greatness.
Pretension never wrote an Iliad, nor drove back Xerxes,
nor christianized the world, nor abolished slavery.

As much virtue as there is, so much appears; as
much goodness as there is, so much reverence it commands. All the devils respect virtue. The high, the generous, the self-devoted sect will always instruct and
command mankind. Never was a sincere word utterly
lost. Never a magnanimity fell to the ground, but there is
some heart to greet and accept it unexpectedly. A man
passes for that he is worth. What he is engraves itself on
his face, on his form, on his fortunes, in letters of light.
Concealment avails him nothing; boasting nothing. There
is confession in the glances of our eyes; in our smiles; in

salutations; and the grasp of hands. His sin bedaubs him, mars all his good impression. Men know not why they do not trust him; but they do not trust him. His vice glasses his eye, cuts lines of mean expression in his cheek, pinches the nose, sets the mark of the beast on the back of the head, and writes O fool! fool! on the forehead of a king.

If you would not be known to do any thing, never do it. A man may play the fool in the drifts of a desert, but every grain of sand shall seem to see. He may be a solitary eater, but he cannot keep his foolish counsel. A broken complexion, a swinish look, ungenerous acts, and the want of due knowledge,—all blab. Can a cook, a Chiffinch, an Iachimo be mistaken for Zeno or Paul? Confucius exclaimed,—"How can a man be concealed! How can a man be concealed!"

On the other hand, the hero fears not, that, if he withhold the avowal of a just and brave act, it will go unwitnessed and unloved. One knows it,—himself,—and is pledged by it to sweetness of peace, and to nobleness of aim, which will prove in the end a better proclamation of it than the relating of the incident. Virtue is the adherence in action to the nature of things, and the nature of things makes it prevalent. It consists in a perpetual substitution of being for seeming, and with sublime propriety God is described as saying, I AM.

The lesson which these observations convey is, Be, and not seem. Let us acquiesce. Let us take our bloated nothingness out of the path of the divine circuits. Let us unlearn our wisdom of the world. Let us lie low in the Lord's power, and learn that truth alone makes rich and great.

If you visit your friend, why need you apologize for not having visited him, and waste his time and deface

your own act? Visit him now. Let him feel that the highest
love has come to see him, in thee, its lowest organ. Or
why need you torment yourself and friend by secret self-
reproaches that you have not assisted him or compli-
mented him with gifts and salutations heretofore? Be a
gift and a benediction. Shine with real light, and not with
the borrowed reflection of gifts. Common men are apologies for men; they bow the head, excuse themselves with
prolix reasons, and accumulate appearances, because the
substance is not.

We are full of these superstitions of sense, the worship of magnitude. We call the poet inactive, because he
is not a president, a merchant, or a porter. We adore an
institution, and do not see that it is founded on a thought
which we have. But real action is in silent moments. The
epochs of our life are not in the visible facts of our choice
of a calling, our marriage, our acquisition of an office,
and the like, but in a silent thought by the way-side as
we walk; in a thought which revises our entire manner of
life, and says,—'Thus hast thou done, but it were better
thus.' And all our after years, like menials, serve and wait
on this, and, according to their ability, execute its will.
This revisal or correction is a constant force, which, as a
tendency, reaches through our lifetime. The object of the
man, the aim of these moments, is to make daylight shine
through him, to suffer the law to traverse his whole being
without obstruction, so that, on what point soever of his
doing your eye falls, it shall report truly of his character,
whether it be his diet, his house, his religious forms, his
society, his mirth, his vote, his opposition. Now he is not
homogeneous, but heterogeneous, and the ray does not
traverse; there are no thorough lights: but the eye of the
beholder is puzzled, detecting many unlike tendencies,
and a life not yet at one.

Why should we make it a point with our false modesty to disparage that man we are, and that form of being
assigned to us? A good man is contented. I love and
honor Epaminondas, but I do not wish to be
Epaminondas. I hold it more just to love the world of this
hour, than the world of his hour. Nor can you, if I am
true, excite me to the least uneasiness by saying, 'He
acted, and thou sittest still.' I see action to be good,
when the need is, and sitting still to be also good.
Epaminondas, if he was the man I take him for, would
have sat still with joy and peace, if his lot had been
mine. Heaven is large, and affords space for all modes of
love and fortitude. Why should we be busybodies and
superserviceable? Action and inaction are alike to the
true. One piece of the tree is cut for a weathercock, and
one for the sleeper of a bridge; the virtue of the wood is
apparent in both.

I desire not to disgrace the soul. The fact that I am
here certainly shows me that the soul had need of an
organ here. Shall I not assume the post? Shall I skulk and
dodge and duck with my unseasonable apologies and
vain modesty, and imagine my being here impertinent?
less pertinent than Epaminondas or Homer being there?
and that the soul did not know its own needs? Besides,
without any reasoning on the matter, I have no discon-
tent. The good soul nourishes me, and unlocks new
magazines of power and enjoyment to me every day. I
will not meanly decline the immensity of good, because I
have heard that it has come to others in another shape.

Besides, why should we be cowed by the name of
Action? 'Tis a trick of the senses,—no more. We know
that the ancestor of every action is a thought. The poor
mind does not seem to itself to be any thing, unless it
have an outside badge,—some Gentoo diet, or Quaker

coat, or Calvinistic prayer-meeting, or philanthropic society, or a great donation, or a high office, or, any how, some wild contrasting action to testify that it is somewhat. The rich mind lies in the sun and sleeps, and is Nature. To think is to act.

Let us, if we must have great actions, make our own so. All action is of an infinite elasticity, and the least admits of being inflated with the celestial air until it eclipses the sun and moon. Let us seek *one* peace by fidelity. Let me heed my duties. Why need I go gadding into the scenes and philosophy of Greek and Italian history, before I have justified myself to my benefactors? How dare I read Washington's campaigns, when I have not answered the letters of my own correspondents? Is not that a just objection to much of our reading? It is a pusillanimous desertion of our work to gaze after our neighbours. It is peeping. Byron says of Jack Bunting,—

"He knew not what to say, and so he swore."

I may say it of our preposterous use of books,—He knew not what to do, and so *he read*. I can think of nothing to fill my time with, and I find the Life of Brant. It is a very extravagant compliment to pay to Brant, or to General Schuyler, or to General Washington. My time should be as good as their time,—my facts, my net of relations, as good as theirs, or either of theirs. Rather let me do my work so well that other idlers, if they choose, may compare my texture with the texture of these and find it identical with the best.

This over-estimate of the possibilities of Paul and Pericles, this under-estimate of our own, comes from a neglect of the fact of an identical nature. Bonaparte knew but one merit, and rewarded in one and the same way the good soldier, the good astronomer, the good poet, the good player. The poet uses the names of Caesar, of Tamerlane, of Bonduca, of Belisarius; the painter uses the conventional story of the Virgin Mary, of Paul, of Peter. He does not, therefore, defer to the nature of these accidental men, of these stock heroes. If the poet write a true drama, then he is Caesar, and not the player of Caesar; then the selfsame strain of thought, emotion as pure, wit as subtle, motions as swift, mounting, extravagant, and a heart as great, self-sufficing, dauntless, which on the waves of its love and hope can uplift all that is reckoned solid and precious in the world,—palaces, gardens, money, navies, kingdoms,—marking its own incomparable worth by the slight it casts on these gauds of men,—these all are his, and by the power of these he rouses the nations. Let a man believe in God, and not in names and places and persons. Let the great soul incarnated in some woman's form, poor and sad and single, in some Dolly or Joan, go out to service, and sweep chambers and scour floors, and its effulgent day beams cannot be muffled or hid, but to sweep and scour will instantly appear supreme and beautiful actions, the top and radiance of human life, and all people will get mops and brooms; until, lo! suddenly the great soul has enshrined itself in some other form, and done some other deed, and that is now the flower and head of all living nature.

We are the photometers, we the irritable goldleaf and tinfoil that measure the accumulations of the subtle element. We know the authentic effects of the true fire through every one of its million disguises.

The Essay
"Circles"

When Emerson reflected in his 1866 journal on the two essential facts for the seeing soul, "I and the Abyss," he might have been describing the geometry of a huge cosmic circle, with "I" at the center and the Abyss an infinite circumference away. He had preceded that journal observation with the stages which approach these facts: "There may be two or three or four steps, according to the genius of each. . . ." In "Circles" he gives us a hint of these steps as we proceed on our journey.

> There are degrees in idealism. We learn first to play with it academically, as the magnet was once a toy. Then we see in the heyday of youth and poetry that it may be true, that it is true in gleams and fragments. Then, its countenance waxes stern and grand, and we see that it must be true. It now shows itself ethical and practical.

At the center of the circle of experience, of the life we build by expanding spirals of thought and action, lies the still point of the turning world, as Eliot phrased it. This center, where the "I" that is the self resides, is also the Universal Order which gives to multiplicity its lawful shape, in this case the circles of existence. On 26

October 1839, Emerson made the following entry in his journal:

> If I should, (or say, *could*) set myself to the unhesitating mission of inviting all persons from house to house to come up into my way of thinking and seeing,—boldly & lovingly affirming the peace which I find in my detached position & perfect reliance on the Universal Order, & demonstrating the contentment & new life & enlarged resources which society would find in the same, that would be occupation, excitement, & the prolific occasion, no doubt of antagonisms, of recontres, & friendships & aversions public & private,—coincidences & collisions with the laws & the law makers, that would elicit deep traits of character in myself & in my fellows.

In "Circles" Emerson explores the "principle of fixture or stability in the soul" which works endlessly to the growth and preservation of Being. What remains frustratingly clear, however, is that we can have no real understanding of or control over how the "eternal generator," as he calls it, will direct our steps.

> I can know that truth is divine and helpful; but how it shall help me I can have no guess, for *so to be* is the sole inlet of *so to know*.

The state of just Being is necessary for the reception of real Knowledge, and the paradox is that Being is that state in which we perceive without self-consciousness. We cannot look directly for guidance, but instead have to trust that once we place ourselves in the stream of power we are carried along to new enlargements of insight and action. The key to this increased capacity is to know that the power does not reside in us, but that we reside in it.

Once we make that subtle but important shift, we are "surprised out of our propriety," as Emerson concludes with both wit and wisdom. We are asked to abandon ourselves to these possibilities, once discrimination tells us that all is well with the chosen path.

CIRCLES

> Nature centres into balls,
> And her proud ephemerals,
> Fast to surface and outside,
> Scan the profile of the sphere;
> Knew they what that signified,
> A new genesis were here.

The eye is the first circle; the horizon which it forms is the second; and throughout nature this primary figure is repeated without end. It is the highest emblem in the cipher of the world. St. Augustine described the nature of God as a circle whose centre was everywhere, and its circumference nowhere. We are all our lifetime reading the copious sense of this first of forms. One moral we have already deduced, in considering the circular or compensatory character of every human action. Another analogy we shall now trace; that every action admits of being outdone. Our life is an apprenticeship to the truth, that around every circle another can be drawn; that there is no end in nature, but every end is a beginning; that there is always another dawn risen on mid-noon, and under every deep a lower deep opens.

This fact, as far as it symbolizes the moral fact of the Unattainable, the flying Perfect, around which the hands of man can never meet, at once the inspirer and the condemner of every success, may conveniently serve us to connect many illustrations of human power in every department.

There are no fixtures in nature. The universe is fluid and volatile. Permanence is but a word of degrees. Our globe seen by God is a transparent law, not a mass of facts. The law dissolves the fact and holds it fluid. Our culture is the predominance of an idea which draws after it this train of cities and institutions. Let us rise into another idea: they will disappear. The Greek sculpture is all melted away, as if it had been statues of ice; here and there a solitary figure or fragment remaining, as we see flecks and scraps of snow left in cold dells and mountain clefts, in June and July. For the genius that created it creates now somewhat else. The Greek letters last a little longer, but are already passing under the same sentence, and tumbling into the inevitable pit which the creation of new thought opens for all that is old. The new continents are built out of the ruins of an old planet; the new races fed out of the decomposition of the foregoing. New arts destroy the old. See the investment of capital in aqueducts made useless by hydraulics; fortifications, by gunpowder; roads and canals, by railways; sails, by steam; steam by electricity.

You admire this tower of granite, weathering the hurts of so many ages. Yet a little waving hand built this huge wall, and that which builds is better than that which is built. The hand that built can topple it down much faster. Better than the hand, and nimbler, was the invisible thought which wrought through it; and thus ever, behind the coarse effect, is a fine cause, which, being narrowly seen, is itself the effect of a finer cause. Every thing looks permanent until its secret is known. A rich estate appears to women a firm and lasting fact; to a merchant, one easily created out of any materials, and easily lost. An

orchard, good tillage, good grounds, seem a fixture, like a
gold mine, or a river, to a citizen; but to a large farmer,
not much more fixed than the state of the crop. Nature
looks provokingly stable and secular, but it has a cause
like all the rest; and when once I comprehend that, will
these fields stretch so immovably wide, these leaves hang
so individually considerable? Permanence is a word of
degrees. Every thing is medial. Moons are no more
bounds to spiritual power than bat-balls.

The key to every man is his thought. Sturdy and
defying though he look, he has a helm which he obeys,
which is the idea after which all his facts are classified.
He can only be reformed by showing him a new idea
which commands his own. The life of man is a self-
evolving circle, which, from a ring imperceptibly small,
rushes on all sides outwards to new and larger circles,
and that without end. The extent to which this generation of circles, wheel without wheel, will go, depends on
the force or truth of the individual soul. For it is the inert
effort of each thought, having formed itself into a circular
wave of circumstance,—as, for instance, an empire, rules
of an art, a local usage, a religious rite,—to heap itself on
that ridge, and to solidify and hem in the life. But if the
soul is quick and strong, it bursts over that boundary on
all sides, and expands another orbit on the great deep,
which also runs up into a high wave, with attempt again
to stop and to bind. But the heart refuses to be imprisoned; in its first and narrowest pulses, it already tends
outward with a vast force, and to immense and innumerable expansions.

Every ultimate fact is only the first of a new series.
Every general law only a particular fact of some more
general law presently to disclose itself. There is no outside, no inclosing wall, no circumference to us. The man

finishes his story,—how good! how final! how it puts a new face on all things! He fills the sky. Lo! on the other side rises also a man, and draws a circle around the circle we had just pronounced the outline of the sphere. Then already is our first speaker not man, but only a first speaker. His only redress is forthwith to draw a circle outside of his antagonist. And so men do by themselves. The result of to-day, which haunts the mind and cannot be escaped, will presently be abridged into a word, and the principle that seemed to explain nature will itself be included as one example of a bolder generalization. In the thought of to-morrow there is a power to upheave all thy creed, all the creeds, all the literatures, of the nations, and marshal thee to a heaven which no epic dream has yet depicted. Every man is not so much a workman in the world, as he is a suggestion of that he should be. Men walk as prophecies of the next age.

Step by step we scale this mysterious ladder: the steps are actions; the new prospect is power. Every several result is threatened and judged by that which follows. Every one seems to be contradicted by the new; it is only limited by the new. The new statement is always hated by the old, and, to those dwelling in the old, comes like an abyss of skepticism. But the eye soon gets wonted to it, for the eye and it are effects of one cause; then its innocency and benefit appear, and presently, all its energy spent, it pales and dwindles before the revelation of the new hour.

Fear not the new generalization. Does the fact look crass and material, threatening to degrade thy theory of spirit? Resist it not; it goes to refine and raise thy theory of matter just as much.

There are no fixtures to men, if we appeal to consciousness. Every man supposes himself not to be fully understood; and if there is any truth in him, if he rests at last on the divine soul, I see not how it can be otherwise. The last chamber, the last closet, he must feel, was never opened; there is always a residuum unknown, unanalyzable. That is, every man believes that he has a greater possibility.

Our moods do not believe in each other. To-day I am full of thoughts, and can write what I please. I see no reason why I should not have the same thought, the same power of expression, to-morrow. What I write, whilst I write it, seems the most natural thing in the world; but yesterday I saw a dreary vacuity in this direction in which now I see so much; and a month hence, I doubt not, I shall wonder who he was that wrote so many continuous pages. Alas for this infirm faith, this will not strenuous, this vast ebb of a vast flow! I am God in nature; I am a weed by the wall.

The continual effort to raise himself above himself, to work a pitch above his last height, betrays itself in a man's relations. We thirst for approbation, yet cannot forgive the approver. The sweet of nature is love; yet, if I have a friend, I am tormented by my imperfections. The love of me accuses the other party. If he were high enough to slight me, then could I love him, and rise by my affection to new heights. A man's growth is seen in the successive choirs of his friends. For every friend whom he loses for truth, he gains a better. I thought, as I walked in the woods and mused on my friends, why should I play with them this game of idolatry? I know and see too well, when not voluntarily blind, the speedy limits of persons called high and worthy. Rich, noble, and great they are by the liberality of our speech, but truth is sad. O blessed Spirit, whom I forsake for these, they are not thou! Every personal consideration that we allow costs us heavenly state. We sell the thrones of angels for a short and turbulent pleasure.

How often must we learn this lesson? Men cease to interest us when we find their limitations. The only sin is limitation. As soon as you once come up with a man's limitations, it is all over with him. Has he talents? has he enterprise? has he knowledge? it boots not. Infinitely alluring and attractive was he to you yesterday, a great hope, a sea to swim in; now, you have found his shores, found it a pond, and you care not if you never see it again.

Each new step we take in thought reconciles twenty seemingly discordant facts, as expressions of one law. Aristotle and Plato are reckoned the respective heads of two schools. A wise man will see that Aristotle Platonizes. By going one step farther back in thought, discordant opinions are reconciled, by being seen to be two extremes of one principle, and we can never go so far back as to preclude a still higher vision.

Beware when the great God lets loose a thinker on this planet. Then all things are at risk. It is as when a conflagration has broken out in a great city, and no man knows what is safe, or where it will end. There is not a piece of science, but its flank may be turned to-morrow; there is not any literary reputation, not the so-called eternal names of fame, that may not be revised and condemned. The very hopes of man, the thoughts of his heart, the religion of nations, the manners and morals of mankind, are all at the mercy of a new generalization. Generalization is always a new influx of the divinity into the mind. Hence the thrill that attends it.

Valor consists in the power of self-recovery, so that a man cannot have his flank turned, cannot be out-generalled, but put him where you will, he stands. This can only be by his preferring truth to his past apprehension of truth; and his alert acceptance of it, from whatever quarter; the intrepid conviction that his laws, his relations to society, his Christianity, his world, may at any time be superseded and decease.

There are degrees in idealism. We learn first to play with it academically, as the magnet was once a toy. Then we see in the heyday of youth and poetry that it may be true, that it is true in gleams and fragments. Then, its countenance waxes stern and grand, and we see that it must be true. It now shows itself ethical and practical. We learn that God IS; that he is in me; and that all things are shadows of him. The idealism of Berkeley is only a crude statement of the idealism of Jesus, and that again is a crude statement of the fact, that all nature is the rapid efflux of goodness executing and organizing itself. Much more obviously is history and the state of the world at any one time directly dependent on the intellectual classification then existing in the minds of men. The things which are dear to men at this hour are so on account of the ideas which have emerged on their mental horizon, and which cause the present order of things as a tree bears its apples. A new degree of culture would instantly revolutionize the entire system of human pursuits.

Conversation is a game of circles. In conversation we pluck up the *termini* which bound the common of silence on every side. The parties are not to be judged by the spirit they partake and even express under this Pentecost. To-morrow they will have receded from this high-water mark. To-morrow you shall find them stooping under the old pack-saddles. Yet let us enjoy the cloven flame whilst it glows on our walls. When each new speaker strikes a new light, emancipates us from the oppression of the last speaker, to oppress us with the greatness and exclusiveness of his own thought, then yields us to another redeemer, we seem to recover our rights, to become men. O, what truths profound and executable only in ages and orbs are supposed in the announcement of every truth! In common hours, society sits cold and statuesque. We all stand waiting, empty,— knowing, possibly, that we can be full, surrounded by mighty symbols which are not symbols to us, but prose and trivial toys. Then cometh the god, and converts the statues into fiery men, and by a flash of his eye burns up the veil which shrouded all things, and the meaning of the very furniture, of cup and saucer, of chair and clock and tester, is manifest. The facts which loomed so large in the fogs of yesterday,—property, climate, breeding, personal beauty, and the like, have strangely changed their proportions. All that we reckoned settled shakes and rattles; and literatures, cities, climates, religions, leave their foundations, and dance before our eyes. And yet here again see the swift circumspection! Good as is discourse, silence is better, and shames it. The length of the discourse indicates the distance of thought betwixt the speaker and the hearer. If they were at a perfect understanding in any part, no words would be necessary thereon. If at one in all parts, no words would be suffered.

Literature is a point outside of our hodiernal circle, through which a new one may be described. The use of literature is to afford us a platform whence we may command a view of our present life, a purchase by which we may move it. We fill ourselves with ancient learning, install ourselves the best we can in Greek, in Punic, in Roman houses, only that we may wiselier see French, English, and American houses and modes of living. In like manner, we see literature best from the midst of wild nature, or from the din of affairs, or from a high religion.

The field cannot be well seen from within the field. The astronomer must have his diameter of the earth's orbit as a base to find the parallax of any star.

Therefore we value the poet. All the argument and all the wisdom is not in the encyclopaedia, or the treatise on metaphysics, or the Body of Divinity, but in the sonnet or the play. In my daily work I incline to repeat my old steps, and do not believe in remedial force, in the power of change and reform. But some Petrarch or Ariosto, filled with the new wine of his imagination, writes me an ode or a brisk romance, full of daring thought and action. He smites and arouses me with his shrill tones, breaks up my whole chain of habits, and I open my eye on my own possibilities. He claps wings to the sides of all the solid old lumber of the world, and I am capable once more of choosing a straight path in theory and practice.

We have the same need to command a view of the religion of the world. We can never see Christianity from the catechism:—from the pastures, from a boat in the pond, from amidst the songs of wood-birds, we possibly may. Cleansed by the elemental light and wind, steeped in the sea of beautiful forms which the field offers us, we may chance to cast a right glance back upon biography. Christianity is rightly dear to the best of mankind; yet was there never a young philosopher whose breeding had fallen into the Christian church, by whom that brave text of Paul's was not specially prized:—"Then shall also the Son be subject unto Him who put all things under him, that God may be all in all." Let the claims and virtues of persons be never so great and welcome, the instinct of man presses eagerly onward to the impersonal and illimitable, and gladly arms itself against the dogmatism of bigots with this generous word outof the book itself.

The natural world may be conceived of as a system of concentric circles, and we now and then detect in nature slight dislocations, which apprize us that this surface on which we now stand is not fixed, but sliding. These manifold tenacious qualities, this chemistry and vegetation, these metals and animals, which seem to stand there for their own sake, are means and methods only,—are words of God, and as fugitive as other words. Has the naturalist or chemist learned his craft, who has explored the gravity of atoms and the elective affinities, who has not yet discerned the deeper law whereof this is only a partial or approximate statement, namely, that like draws to like; and that the goods which belong to you gravitate to you, and need not be pursued with pains and cost? Yet is that statement approximate also, and not final. Omnipresence is a higher fact. Not through subtle, subterranean channels need friend and fact be drawn to their counterpart, but, rightly considered, these things proceed from the eternal generation of the soul. Cause and effect are two sides of one fact.

The same law of eternal procession ranges all that we call the virtues, and extinguishes each in the light of a better. The great man will not be prudent in the popular sense; all his prudence will be so much deduction from his grandeur. But it behooves each to see, when he sacrifices prudence, to what god he devotes it; if to ease and pleasure, he had better be prudent still; if to a great trust, he can well spare his mule and panniers who has a winged chariot instead. Geoffrey draws on his boots to go through the woods, that his feet may be safer from the bite of snakes; Aaron never thinks of such a peril. In many years neither is harmed by such an accident. Yet it seems to me, that, with every precaution you take against such an evil, you put yourself into the power of the evil.

I suppose that the highest prudence is the lowest prudence. Is this too sudden a rushing from the centre to the verge of our orbit? Think how many times we shall fall back into pitiful calculations before we take up our rest in the great sentiment, or make the verge of to-day the new centre. Besides, your bravest sentiment is familiar to the humblest men. The poor and the low have their way of expressing the last facts of philosophy as well as you. "Blessed be nothing," and "the worse things are, the better they are," are proverbs which express the transcendentalism of common life.

One man's justice is another's injustice; one man's beauty, another's ugliness; one man's wisdom, another's folly; as one beholds the same objects from a higher point. One man thinks justice consists in paying debts, and has no measure in his abhorrence of another who is very remiss in this duty, and makes the creditor wait tediously. But that second man has his own way of looking at things; asks himself which debt must I pay first, the debt to the rich, or the debt to the poor? the debt of money, or the debt of thought to mankind, of genius to nature? For you, O broker! there is no other principle but arithmetic. For me, commerce is of trivial import; love, faith, truth of character, the aspiration of man, these are sacred; nor can I detach one duty, like you, from all other duties, and concentrate my forces mechanically on the payment of moneys. Let me live onward; you shall find that, though slower, the progress of my character will liquidate all these debts without injustice to higher claims. If a man should dedicate himself to the payment of notes, would not this be injustice? Does he owe no debt but money? And are all claims on him to be postponed to a landlord's or a banker's?

There is no virtue which is final; all are initial. The

virtues of society are vices of the saint. The terror of reform is the discovery that we must cast away our virtues, or what we have always esteemed such, into the same pit that has consumed our grosser vices .

"Forgive his crimes, forgive his virtues too,
Those smaller faults, half converts to the right."

It is the highest power of divine moments that they abolish our contritions also. I accuse myself of sloth and unprofitableness day by day; but when these waves of God flow into me, I no longer reckon lost time. I no longer poorly compute my possible achievement by what remains to me of the month or the year; for these moments confer a sort of omnipresence and omnipotence which asks nothing of duration, but sees that the energy of the mind is commensurate with the work to be done, without time.

And thus, O circular philosopher, I hear some reader exclaim, you have arrived at a fine Pyrrhonism, at an equivalence and indifferency of all actions, and would fain teach us that, *if we are true*, forsooth, our crimes may be lively stones out of which we shall construct the temple of the true God!

I am not careful to justify myself. I own I am gladdened by seeing the predominance of the saccharine principle throughout vegetable nature, and not less by beholding in morals that unrestrained inundation of the principle of good into every chink and hole that selfishness has left open, yea, into selfishness and sin itself; so that no evil is pure, nor hell itself without its extreme satisfactions. But lest I should mislead any when I have my own head and obey my whims, let me remind the reader that I am only an experimenter. Do not set the least value on what I do, or the least discredit on what I do not, as if

I pretended to settle any thing as true or false. I unsettle all things. No facts are to me sacred; none are profane; I simply experiment, an endless seeker, with no Past at my back.

Yet this incessant movement and progression which all things partake could never become sensible to us but by contrast to some principle of fixture or stability in the soul. Whilst the eternal generation of circles proceeds, the eternal generator abides. That central life is somewhat superior to creation, superior to knowledge and thought, and contains all its circles. For ever it labors to create a life and thought as large and excellent as itself; but in vain; for that which is made instructs how to make a better.

Thus there is no sleep, no pause, no preservation, but all things renew, germinate, and spring. Why should we import rags and relics into the new hour? Nature abhors the old, and old age seems the only disease; all others run into this one. We call it by many names,— fever, intemperance, insanity, stupidity, and crime; they are all forms of old age; they are rest, conservatism, appropriation, inertia, not newness, not the way onward. We grizzle every day. I see no need of it. Whilst we converse with what is above us, we do not grow old, but grow young. Infancy, youth, receptive, aspiring, with religious eye looking upward, counts itself nothing, and abandons itself to the instruction flowing from all sides. But the man and woman of seventy assume to know all, they have outlived their hope, they renounce aspiration, accept the actual for the necessary, and talk down to the young. Let them, then, become organs of the Holy Ghost; let them be lovers; let them behold truth; and their eyes are uplifted, their wrinkles smoothed, they are perfumed again with hope and power. This old age ought not to creep on a human mind. In nature every moment is new; the past is always swallowed and forgotten; the coming only is sacred. Nothing is secure but life, transition, the energizing spirit. No love can be bound by oath or covenant to secure it against a higher love. No truth so sublime but it may be trivial to-morrow in the light of new thoughts. People wish to be settled; only as far as they are unsettled is there any hope for them.

Life is a series of surprises. We do not guess to-day the mood, the pleasure, the power of to-morrow, when we are building up our being. Of lower states,—of acts of routine and sense,—we can tell somewhat; but the masterpieces of God, the total growths and universal movements of the soul, he hideth; they are incalculable. I can know that truth is divine and helpful; but how it shall help me I can have no guess, for *so to be* is the sole inlet of *so to know*. The new position of the advancing man has all the powers of the old, yet has them all new. It carries in its bosom all the energies of the past, yet is itself an exhalation of the morning. I cast a way in this new moment all my once hoarded knowledge, as vacant and vain. Now, for the first time, seem I to know any thing rightly. The simplest words,—we do not know what they mean, except when we love and aspire.

The difference between talents and character is adroitness to keep the old and trodden round, and power and courage to make a new road to new and better goals. Character makes an overpowering present; a cheerful, determined hour, which fortifies all the company, by making them see that much is possible and excellent that was not thought of. Character dulls the impression of particular events. When we see the conqueror, we do not think much of any one battle or success. We see that we had exaggerated the difficulty. It was easy to him. The great man is not convulsible or tormentable; events pass over him without much impression. People say sometimes, 'See what I have overcome; see how cheerful I am; see how completely I have triumphed over these black events.' Not if they still remind me of the black event. True conquest is the causing the calamity to fade and disappear, as an early cloud of insignificant result in a history so large and advancing.

The one thing which we seek with insatiable desire is to forget ourselves, to be surprised out of our propriety, to lose our sempiternal memory, and to do something without knowing how or why; in short, to draw a new circle. Nothing great was ever achieved without enthusiasm. The way of life is wonderful: it is by abandonment. The great moments of history are the facilities of performance through the strength of ideas, as the works of genius and religion. "A man," said Oliver Cromwell, "never rises so high as when he knows not whither he is going." Dreams and drunkenness, the use of opium and alcohol are the semblance and counterfeit of this oracular genius, and hence their dangerous attraction for men. For the like reason, they ask the aid of wild passions, as in gaming and war, to ape in some manner these flames and generosities of the heart.

The Essay "Experience"

For this volume, I have saved "Experience" for last because it is at once the most discouraging and most helpful statement Emerson ever made. It is discouraging because in case we thought that living the examined life and recovering some of the perceptions we have lost was going to be easy, Emerson here locates us firmly in the reality of the struggle. We exist in an overwhelming deluge of illusions in the repetitious, sense-driven, unconscious passage of daily life. In that daily life we focus primarily on getting and spending, on managing and coping, on reacting to stimuli, that we perceive to be demands on our time and threats to our security and well-being. Most of our days are spent making our way in the world, sustaining a certain momentum we began years ago, all the while losing by degrees any sense of how we started or where we are going. We have created elaborate illusions of personal identity, self-worth, relationships, meanings and reasons for things. We hold stubbornly to opinions about what is important, interesting, true, beautiful, and relevant to our existence. And when someone or something challenges those illusory opinions, we fight to the death—or at least to the point of exhaustion—to preserve them. That is insanity, and we live it every day in a kind of drugged sleep.

Recovery from such insanity is not easy, and "Experience" lays out the ground rules for the struggle. First, Emerson tells us that we are driven by mood more than fact. Grief, he tells us, is temporary and shallow. The soul is not touched. In a rare personal observation, Emerson tells us that even when he lost his son, he seemed to have lost a beautiful estate, no more. We might attribute these assertions to a certain coldness in Emerson's personality, but there is ample evidence, particularly in the journals and letters, of the grim melancholy which gripped him through the many deaths he faced in his life. However, despite the depth of his feelings, indeed, through them, he was able to observe those feelings and to isolate them from his perceptions. The point is that the detachment he describes is essential to eventual sanity and self-recovery.

The help Emerson provides lies in documenting with great honesty the illusory nature of our ordinary experience. Most of our experience is illusion: "The pith of each man's genius is contracted to a very few hours." The transparent eyeball experience described in *Nature* was such an hour. Our task is to use the reality of those few hours to fuel our days and to guide us when the power of illusion seems overwhelming.

The next step is to understand that "we live amid surfaces, and the true art of life is to skate well on them." As Emerson points out, the objects of our existence have about them a lubricity which makes grasping them impossible. Nature is, in fact, so slippery that we are not given "a berry for our philosophy." All of our approaches to the truth are oblique. These images suggest that the dialectic of inquiry is always indirect, sly even, as if the secrets of nature are consciously kept from us. There is great power to be drawn from the recesses of nature, as we learned so vividly in the release of atomic energy. But Emerson is quick to qualify that conclusion when he says, "but I have not found that much was gained by manipular attempts to realize the world of thought."

Since Surface and Illusion are two of Emerson's Lords of Life—along with Temperament, Succession, Surprise, Reality, and Subjectiveness—we begin to see the extent to which we are surrounded by these power-ful forces. No wonder achieving some degree of clarity is so difficult. Much is accomplished, however, by the trick, or perhaps it is a philosophical truth, of seeing these so-called Lords for what they are: creations arising out of the mental life of human beings in response to living. They are the same as the Fall of Man, as Emerson says.

Any working-through of experience which allows us to see with greater clarity and honesty helps us reach new levels of understanding. When we are presented with an insight, when the moment is illuminated only slightly by a certain presence in the mind, we have the capacity to remember the moment and to extend similar moments a bit longer. And so we progress. Emerson says of this moment of clarity, "I do not make it; I arrive there and behold what was there already." The affirmation that behind all the veils of illusion exists a sublime order with which we actively participate is Emerson's triumphant vision. The result of that participation is "the transforma-tion of genius into practical power."

EXPERIENCE

The lords of life, the lords of life,—
I saw them pass,
In their own guise,
Like and unlike,
Portly and grim,
Use and Surprise,
Surface and Dream,
Succession swift, and spectral Wrong,
Temperament without a tongue,
And the inventor of the game
Omnipresent without name;—
Some to see, some to be guessed,
They marched from east to west:
Little man, least of all,
Among the legs of his guardians tall,
Walked about with puzzled look:—
Him by the hand dear nature took;
Dearest nature, strong and kind,
Whispered, 'Darling, never mind!
Tomorrow they will wear another face,
The founder thou! these are thy race!'

Where do we find ourselves? In a series of which we
do not know the extremes, and believe that it has none.
We wake and find ourselves on a stair; there are stairs
below us, which we seem to have ascended; there are
stairs above us, many a one, which go upward and out of
sight. But the Genius which, according to the old belief,
stands at the door by which we enter, and gives us the
lethe to drink, that we may tell no tales, mixed the cup too
strongly, and we cannot shake off the lethargy now at
noonday. Sleep lingers all our lifetime about our eyes, as

night hovers all day in the boughs of the fir-tree. All things swim and glitter. Our life is not so much threatened as our perception. Ghostlike we glide through nature, and should not know our place again. Did our birth fall in some fit of indigence and frugality in nature, that she was so sparing of her fire and so liberal of her earth, that it appears to us that we lack the affirmative principle, and though we have health and reason, yet we have no superfluity of spirit for new creation? We have enough to live and bring the year about, but not an ounce to impart or to invest. Ah that our Genius were a little more of a genius! We are like millers on the lower levels of a stream, when the factories above them have exhausted the water. We too fancy that the upper people must have raised their dams.

If any of us knew what we were doing, or where we are going, then when we think we best know! We do not know today whether we are busy or idle. In times when we thought ourselves indolent, we have afterwards discovered, that much was accomplished, and much was begun in us. All our days are so unprofitable while they pass, that 'tis wonderful where or when we ever got anything of this which we call wisdom, poetry, virtue. We never got it on any dated calendar day. Some heavenly days must have been intercalated somewhere, like those that Hermes won with dice of the Moon, that Osiris might be born. It is said, all martyrdoms looked mean when they were suffered. Every ship is a romantic object, except that we sail in. Embark, and the romance quits our vessel, and hangs on every other sail in the horizon. Our life looks trivial, and we shun to record it. Men seem to have learned of the horizon the art of perpetual retreating and reference. 'Yonder uplands are rich pasturage, and my neighbor has fertile meadow, but my field,' says the querulous farmer, 'only holds the world together.' I quote another man's saying; unluckily, that other withdraws himself in the same way, and quotes me. 'Tis the trick of nature thus to degrade today; a good deal of buzz, and somewhere a result slipped magically in. Every roof is agreeable to the eye, until it is lifted; then we find tragedy and moaning women, and hard-eyed husbands, and deluges of lethe, and the men ask, 'What's the news?' as if the old were so bad. How many individuals can we count in society? how many actions? how many opinions? So much of our time is preparation, so much is routine, and so much retrospect, that the pith of each man's genius contracts itself to a very few hours. The history of literature—take the net result of Tiraboschi, Warton, or Schlegel,—is a sum of very few ideas, and of very few original tales,—all the rest being variation of these. So in this great society wide lying around us, a critical analysis would find very few sponta-neous actions. It is almost all custom and gross sense. There are even few opinions, and these seem organic in the speakers, and do not disturb the universal necessity.

What opium is instilled into all disaster! It shows for-midable as we approach it, but there is at last no rough rasping friction, but the most slippery sliding surfaces. We fall soft on a thought. *Ate Dea* is gentle,

> "Over men's heads walking aloft,
> With tender feet treading so soft."

People grieve and bemoan themselves, but it is not half so bad with them as they say. There are moods in which we court suffering, in the hope that here, at least, we shall find reality, sharp peaks and edges of truth. But it turns out to be scene-painting and counterfeit. The only thing grief has taught me, is to know how shallow it is. That, like all the rest, plays about the surface, and never introduces me into the reality, for contact with which, we would even pay the costly price of sons and lovers. Was it Boscovich who found out that bodies never come in contact? Well, souls never touch their objects. An innavigable sea washes with silent waves between us and the things we aim at and converse with. Grief too will make us idealists. In the death of my son, now more than two years ago, I seem to have lost a beautiful estate,—no more. I cannot get it nearer to me. If tomorrow I should be informed of the bankruptcy of my principal debtors, the loss of my property would be a great inconvenience to me, perhaps, for many years; but it would leave me as it found me,—neither better nor worse. So is it with this calamity: it does not touch me: some thing which I fancied was a part of me, which could not be torn away without tearing me, nor enlarged without enriching me, falls off from me, and leaves no scar. It was caducous. I grieve that grief can teach me nothing, nor carry me one step into real nature. The Indian who was laid under a curse, that the wind should not blow on him, nor water flow to him, nor fire burn him, is a type of us all. The dearest events are summer-rain, and we the Para coats that shed every drop. Nothing is left us now but death. We look to that with a grim satisfaction, saying, there at least is reality that will not dodge us.

I take this evanescence and lubricity of all objects, which lets them slip through our fingers then when we clutch hardest, to be the most unhandsome part of our condition. Nature does not like to be observed, and likes that we should be her fools and playmates. We may have the sphere for our cricket-ball, but not a berry for our philosophy. Direct strokes she never gave us power to make; all our blows glance, all our hits are accidents. Our relations to each other are oblique and casual.

Dream delivers us to dream, and there is no end to illusion. Life is a train of moods like a string of beads, and, as we pass through them, they prove to be many-colored lenses which paint the world their own hue, and each shows only what lies in its focus. From the mountain you see the mountain. We animate what we can, and we see only what we animate. Nature and books belong to the eyes that see them. It depends on the mood of the man, whether he shall see the sunset or the fine poem. There are always sunsets, and there is always genius; but only a few hours so serene that we can relish nature or criticism. The more or less depends on structure or temperament. Temperament is the iron wire on which the beads are strung. Of what use is fortune or talent to a cold and defective nature? Who cares what sensibility or discrimination a man has at some time shown, if he falls asleep in his chair? or if he laugh and giggle? or if he apologize? or is affected with egotism? or thinks of his dollar? or cannot go by food? or has gotten a child in his boyhood? Of what use is genius, if the organ is too convex or too concave, and cannot find a focal distance within the actual horizon of human life? Of what use, if the brain is too cold or too hot, and the man does not care enough for results, to stimulate him to experiment, and hold him up in it? or if the web is too finely woven, too irritable by pleasure and pain, so that life stagnates from too much reception, without due outlet? Of what use to make heroic vows of amendment, if the same old law-breaker is to keep them? What cheer can the religious sentiment yield, when that is suspected to be secretly dependent on the seasons of the year, and the state of the blood? I knew a witty physician who found theology in the biliary duct, and used to affirm that if there was disease in the liver, the man became a

Calvinist, and if that organ was sound, he became a Unitarian. Very mortifying is the reluctant experience that some unfriendly excess or imbecility neutralizes the promise of genius. We see young men who owe us a new world, so readily and lavishly they promise, but they never acquit the debt; they die young and dodge the account: or if they live, they lose themselves in the crowd.

Temperament also enters fully into the system of illusions, and shuts us in a prison of glass which we cannot see. There is an optical illusion about every person we meet. In truth, they are all creatures of given temperament, which will appear in a given character, whose boundaries they will never pass: but we look at them, they seem alive, and we presume there is impulse in them. In the moment it seems impulse; in the year, in the lifetime, it turns out to be a certain uniform tune which the revolving barrel of the music-box must play. Men resist the conclusion in the morning, but adopt it as the evening wears on, that temper prevails over everything of time, place, and condition, and is inconsumable in the flames of religion. Some modifications the moral sentiment avails to impose, but the individual texture holds its dominion, if not to bias the moral judgments, yet to fix the measure of activity and of enjoyment.

I thus express the law as it is read from the platform of ordinary life, but must not leave it without noticing the capital exception. For temperament is a power which no man willingly hears any one praise but himself. On the platform of physics, we cannot resist the contracting influences of so-called science. Temperament puts all divinity to rout. I know the mental proclivity of physicians. I hear the chuckle of the phrenologists. Theoretic kidnappers and slave-drivers, they esteem each man the

victim of another, who winds him round his finger by
knowing the law of his being, and by such cheap sign-
boards as the color of his beard, or the slope of his
occiput, reads the inventory of his fortunes and character.
The grossest ignorance does not disgust like this impu-
dent knowingness. The physicians say, they are not
materialists; but they are:—Spirit is matter reduced to an
extreme thinness: O *so* thin!—But the definition of *spiritual* should be, *that which is its own evidence*. What
notions do they attach to love! what to religion! One
would not willingly pronounce these words in their hearing, and give them the occasion to profane them. I saw a
gracious gentleman who adapts his conversation to the
form of the head of the man he talks with! I had fancied
that the value of life lay in its inscrutable possibilities; in
the fact that I never know, in addressing myself to a new
individual, what may befall me. I carry the keys of my
castle in my hand, ready to throw them at the feet of my
lord, whenever and in what disguise soever he shall
appear. I know he is in the neighborhood hidden among
vagabonds. Shall I preclude my future, by taking a high
seat, and kindly adapting my conversation to the shape
of heads? When I come to that, the doctors shall buy me
for a cent.—'But, sir, medical history; the report to the
Institute; the proven facts!'—I distrust the facts and the
inferences. Temperament is the veto or limitation-power
in the constitution, very justly applied to restrain an
opposite excess in the constitution, but absurdly offered
as a bar to original equity. When virtue is in presence, all
subordinate powers sleep. On its own level, or in view of
nature, temperament is final. I see not, if one be once
caught in this trap of so-called sciences, any escape for
the man from the links of the chain of physical necessity.
Given such an embryo, such a history must follow. On

this platform, one lives in a sty of sensualism, and would soon come to suicide. But it is impossible that the creative power should exclude itself. Into every intelligence there is a door which is never closed, through which the creator passes. The intellect, seeker of absolute truth, or the heart, lover of absolute good, intervenes for our succor, and at one whisper of these high powers, we awake from ineffectual struggles with this nightmare. We hurl it into its own hell, and cannot again contract ourselves to so base a state.

The secret of the illusoriness is in the necessity of a succession of moods or objects. Gladly we would anchor, but the anchorage is quicksand. This onward trick of nature is too strong for us: *Pero si muove*. When, at night, I look at the moon and stars, I seem stationary, and they to hurry. Our love of the real draws us to permanence, but health of body consists in circulation, and sanity of mind in variety or facility of association. We need change of objects. Dedication to one thought is quickly odious. We house with the insane, and must humor them; then conversation dies out. Once I took such delight in Montaigne, that I thought I should not need any other book; before that, in Shakspeare; then in Plutarch; then in Plotinus; at one time in Bacon; afterwards in Goethe; even in Bettine; but now I turn the pages of either of them languidly, whilst I still cherish their genius. So with pictures; each will bear an emphasis of attention once, which it cannot retain, though we fain would continue to be pleased in that manner. How strongly I have felt of pictures, that when you have seen one well, you must take your leave of it; you shall never see it again. I have had good lessons from pictures, which I have since seen without emotion or remark. A deduction must be made from the opinion, which even the wise express of a new book or occurrence. Their opinion gives me tidings of their mood, and some vague guess at the new fact but is nowise to be trusted as the lasting relation between that intellect and that thing. The child asks, 'Mamma, why don't I like the story as well as when you told it me yesterday?' Alas, child, it is even so with the oldest cherubim of knowledge. But will it answer thy question to say, Because thou wert born to a whole, and this story is a particular? The reason of the pain this discovery causes us (and we make it late in respect to works of art and intellect), is the plaint of tragedy which murmurs from it in regard to persons, to friendship and love.

That immobility and absence of elasticity which we find in the arts, we find with more pain in the artist. There is no power of expansion in men. Our friends early appear to us as representatives of certain ideas, which they never pass or exceed. They stand on the brink of the ocean of thought and power, but they never take the single step that would bring them there. A man is like a bit of Labrador spar, which has no lustre as you turn it in your hand, until you come to a particular angle; then it shows deep and beautiful colors. There is no adaptation or universal applicability in men, but each has his special talent, and the mastery of successful men consists in adroitly keeping themselves where and when that turn shall be oftenest to be practised. We do what we must, and call it by the best names we can, and would fain have the praise of having intended the result which ensues. I cannot recall any form of man who is not superfluous sometimes. But is not this pitiful? Life is not worth the taking, to do tricks in.

Of course, it needs the whole society, to give the

symmetry we seek. The parti-colored wheel must revolve very fast to appear white. Something is learned too by conversing with so much folly and defect. In fine, whoever loses, we are always of the gaining party. Divinity is behind our failures and follies also. The plays of children are nonsense, but very educative nonsense. So it is with the largest and solemnest things, with commerce, government, church, marriage, and so with the history of every man's bread, and the ways by which he is to come by it. Like a bird which alights nowhere, but hops perpetually from bough to bough, is the Power which abides in no man and in no woman, but for a moment speaks from this one, and for another moment from that one.

But what help from these fineries or pedantries? What help from thought? Life is not dialectics. We, I think, in these times, have had lessons enough of the futility of criticism. Our young people have thought and written much on labor and reform, and for all that they have written, neither the world nor themselves have got on a step. Intellectual tasting of life will not supersede muscular activity. If a man should consider the nicety of the passage of a piece of bread down his throat, he would starve. At Education-Farm, the noblest theory of life sat on the noblest figures of young men and maidens, quite powerless and melancholy. It would not rake or pitch a ton of hay; it would not rub down a horse; and the men and maidens it left pale and hungry. A political orator wittily compared our party promises to western roads, which opened stately enough, with planted trees on either side, to tempt the traveller, but soon became narrow and narrower, and ended in a squirrel-track, and ran up a tree. So does culture with us; it ends in headache. Unspeakably sad and barren does life look to

those, who a few months ago were dazzled with the
splendor of the promise of the times. "There is now no
longer any right course of action, nor any self-devotion
left among the Iranis." Objections and criticism we have
had our fill of. There are objections to every course of
life and action, and the practical wisdom infers an indifferency, from the omnipresence of objection. The whole
frame of things preaches indifferency. Do not craze yourself with thinking, but go about your business anywhere.
Life is not intellectual or critical, but sturdy. Its chief good
is for well-mixed people who can enjoy what they find,
without question. Nature hates peeping, and our mothers
speak her very sense when they say, "Children, eat your
victuals, and say no more of it." To fill the hour,—that is
happiness; to fill the hour, and leave no crevice for a
repentance or an approval. We live amid surfaces, and
the true art of life is to skate well on them. Under the
oldest mouldiest conventions, a man of native force prospers just as well as in the newest world, and that by skill
of handling and treatment. He can take hold anywhere.
Life itself is a mixture of power and form, and will not
bear the least excess of either. To finish the moment, to
find the journey's end in every step of the road, to live
the greatest number of good hours, is wisdom. It is not
the part of men, but of fanatics, or of mathematicians, if
you will, to say, that, the shortness of life considered, it is
not worth caring whether for so short a duration we
were sprawling in want, or sitting high. Since our office
is with moments, let us husband them. Five minutes of
today are worth as much to me, as five minutes in the
next millennium. Let us be poised, and wise, and our
own, today. Let us treat the men and women well: treat
them as if they were real: perhaps they are. Men live in
their fancy, like drunkards whose hands are too soft and

tremulous for successful labor. It is a tempest of fancies, and the only ballast I know, is a respect to the present hour. Without any shadow of doubt, amidst this vertigo of shows and politics, I settle myself ever the firmer in the creed, that we should not postpone and refer and wish, but do broad justice where we are, by whomsoever we deal with, accepting our actual companions and circumstances, however humble or odious, as the mystic officials to whom the universe has delegated its whole pleasure for us. If these are mean and malignant, their contentment, which is the last victory of justice, is a more satisfying echo to the heart, than the voice of poets and the casual sympathy of admirable persons. I think that however a thoughtful man may suffer from the defects and absurdities of his company, he cannot without affectation deny to any set of men and women, a sensibility to extraordinary merit. The coarse and frivolous have an instinct of superiority, if they have not a sympathy, and honor it in their blind capricious way with sincere homage.

The fine young people despise life, but in me, and in such as with me are free from dyspepsia, and to whom a day is a sound and solid good, it is a great excess of politeness to look scornful and to cry for company. I am grown by sympathy a little eager and sentimental, but leave me alone, and I should relish every hour and what it brought me, the pot-luck of the day, as heartily as the oldest gossip in the bar-room. I am thankful for small mercies. I compared notes with one of my friends who expects everything of the universe, and is disappointed when anything is less than the best, and I found that I begin at the other extreme, expecting nothing, and am always full of thanks for moderate goods. I accept the clangor and jangle of contrary tendencies. I find my account in sots and bores also. They give a reality to the circumjacent picture, which such a vanishing meteorous appearance can ill spare. In the morning I awake, and find the old world, wife, babes, and mother, Concord and Boston, the dear old spiritual world, and even the dear old devil not far off. If we will take the good we find, asking no questions, we shall have heaping measures. The great gifts are not got by analysis. Everything good is on the highway. The middle region of our being is the temperate zone. We may climb into the thin and cold realm of pure geometry and lifeless science, or sink into that of sensation. Between these extremes is the equator of life, of thought, of spirit, of poetry,—a narrow belt. Moreover, in popular experience, everything good is on the highway. A collector peeps into all the picture-shops of Europe, for a landscape of Poussin, a crayon-sketch of Salvator; but the Transfiguration, the Last Judgment, the Communion of St. Jerome, and what are as transcendent as these, are on the walls of the Vatican, the Uffizii, or the Louvre, where every footman may see them; to say nothing of nature's pictures in every street, of sunsets and sunrises every day, and the sculpture of the human body never absent. A collector recently bought at public auction, in London, for one hundred and fifty-seven guineas, an autograph of Shakspeare: but for nothing a school-boy can read Hamlet, and can detect secrets of highest concernment yet unpublished therein. I think I will never read any but the commonest books,—the Bible, Homer, Dante, Shakspeare, and Milton. Then we are impatient of so public a life and planet, and run hither and thither for nooks and secrets. The imagination delights in the wood-craft of Indians, trappers, and bee-hunters. We fancy that we are strangers, and not so intimately domesticated in the planet as the wild man, and the wild beast and bird. But the exclusion reaches them also; reaches the climbing, flying, gliding, feathered and four-footed man. Fox and woodchuck, hawk and snipe, and bittern, when nearly seen, have no more root in the deep world than man, and are just such superficial tenants of the globe. Then the new molecular philosophy shows astronomical interspaces betwixt atom and atom, shows that the world is all outside: it has no inside.

The mid-world is best. Nature, as we know her, is no saint. The lights of the church, the ascetics, Gentoos and Grahamites, she does not distinguish by any favor. She comes eating and drinking and sinning. Her darlings, the great, the strong, the beautiful, are not children of our law, do not come out of the Sunday School, nor weigh their food, nor punctually keep the commandments. If we will be strong with her strength, we must not harbor such disconsolate consciences, borrowed too from the consciences of other nations. We must set up the strong present tense against all the rumors of wrath, past or to come. So many things are unsettled which it is of the first importance to settle,—and, pending their settlement, we will do as we do. Whilst the debate goes forward on the equity of commerce, and will not be closed for a century or two, New and Old England may keep shop. Law of copyright and international copyright is to be discussed, and, in the interim, we will sell our books for the most we can. Expediency of literature, reason of literature, lawfulness of writing down a thought, is questioned; much is to say on both sides, and, while the fight waxes hot, thou, dearest scholar, stick to thy foolish task, add a line every hour, and between whiles add a line. Right to hold land, right of property, is disputed, and the conventions convene, and before the vote is taken, dig

away in your garden, and spend your earnings as a waif
or godsend to all serene and beautiful purposes. Life
itself is a bubble and a skepticism, and a sleep within a
sleep. Grant it, and as much more as they will,—but
thou, God's darling! heed thy private dream: thou wilt
not be missed in the scorning and skepticism: there are
enough of them: stay there in thy closet, and toil, until
the rest are agreed what to do about it. Thy sickness,
they say, and thy puny habit, require that thou do this or
avoid that, but know that thy life is a flitting state, a tent
for a night, and do thou, sick or well, finish that stint.
Thou art sick, but shalt not be worse, and the universe,
which holds thee dear, shall be the better.

   Human life is made up of the two elements, power
and form, and the proportion must be invariably kept, if
we would have it sweet and sound. Each of these elements in excess makes a mischief as hurtful as its defect.
Everything runs to excess: every good quality is noxious,
if unmixed, and, to carry the danger to the edge of ruin,
nature causes each man's peculiarity to superabound.
Here, among the farms, we adduce the scholars as examples of this treachery. They are nature's victims of
expression. You who see the artist, the orator, the poet,
too near, and find their life no more excellent than that
of mechanics or farmers, and themselves victims of partiality, very hollow and haggard, and pronounce them
failures,—not heroes, but quacks,—conclude very rea-
sonably, that these arts are not for man, but are disease.
Yet nature will not bear you out. Irresistible nature made
men such, and makes legions more of such, every day.
You love the boy reading in a book, gazing at a drawing,
or a cast: yet what are these millions who read and
behold, but incipient writers and sculptors? Add a little
more of that quality which now reads and sees, and they

will seize the pen and chisel. And if one remembers how
innocently he began to be an artist, he perceives that
nature joined with his enemy. A man is a golden impossibility. The line he must walk is a hair's breadth. The
wise through excess of wisdom is made a fool.

How easily, if fate would suffer it, we might keep
forever these beautiful limits, and adjust ourselves, once
for all, to the perfect calculation of the kingdom of
known cause and effect. In the street and in the news-
papers, life appears so plain a business, that manly resolution and adherence to the multiplication-table through
all weathers, will insure success. But ah! presently comes
a day, or is it only a half-hour, with its angel-whisper-
ing,—which discomfits the conclusions of nations and of
years! Tomorrow again, everything looks real and angu-
lar, the habitual standards are reinstated, common sense
is as rare as genius,—is the basis of genius, and experience is hands and feet to every enterprise;—and yet, he
who should do his business on this understanding,
would be quickly bankrupt. Power keeps quite another
road than the turnpikes of choice and will, namely, the
subterranean and invisible tunnels and channels of life. It
is ridiculous that we are diplomatists, and doctors, and
considerate people: there are no dupes like these. Life is
a series of surprises, and would not be worth taking or
keeping, if it were not. God delights to isolate us every
day, and hide from us the past and the future. We would
look about us, but with grand politeness he draws down
before us an impenetrable screen of purest sky, and
another behind us of purest sky. 'You will not remember,' he seems to say, 'and you will not expect.' All good
conversation, manners, and action, come from a spon-
taneity which forgets usages, and makes the moment

great. Nature hates calculators; her methods are saltatory and impulsive. Man lives by pulses; our organic movements are such; and the chemical and ethereal agents are undulatory and alternate; and the mind goes antagonizing on, and never prospers but by fits. We thrive by casualties. Our chief experiences have been casual. The most attractive class of people are those who are powerful obliquely, and not by the direct stroke: men of genius, but not yet accredited: one gets the cheer of their light, without paying too great a tax. Theirs is the beauty of the bird, or the morning light, and not of art. In the thought of genius there is always a surprise; and the moral sentiment is well called "the newness," for it is never other; as new to the oldest intelligence as to the young child,— "the kingdom that cometh without observation." In like manner, for practical success, there must not be too much design. A man will not be observed in doing that which he can do best. There is a certain magic about his properest action, which stupefies your powers of observation, so that though it is done before you, you wist not of it. The art of life has a pudency, and will not be exposed. Every man is an impossibility, until he is born; every thing impossible, until we see a success. The ardors of piety agree at last with the coldest skepticism,—that nothing is of us or our works,—that all is of God. Nature will not spare us the smallest leaf of laurel. All writing comes by the grace of God, and all doing and having. I would gladly be moral, and keep due metes and bounds, which I dearly love, and allow the most to the will of man, but I have set my heart on honesty in this chapter, and I can see nothing at last, in success or failure, than more or less of vital force supplied from the Eternal. The results of life are uncalculated and uncalculable. The years teach much which the days never know.

The persons who compose our company, converse, and come and go, and design and execute many things, and somewhat comes of it all, but an unlooked for result. The individual is always mistaken. He designed many things, and drew in other persons as coadjutors, quarrelled with some or all, blundered much, and something is done; all are a little advanced, but the individual is always mistaken. It turns out somewhat new, and very unlike what he promised himself.

The ancients, struck with this irreducibleness of the elements of human life to calculation, exalted Chance into a divinity, but that is to stay too long at the spark,— which glitters truly at one point,—but the universe is warm with the latency of the same fire. The miracle of life which will not be expounded, but will remain a miracle, introduces a new element. In the growth of the embryo, Sir Everard Home, I think, noticed that the evolution was not from one central point, but co-active from three or more points. Life has no memory. That which proceeds in succession might be remembered, but that which is coexistent, or ejaculated from a deeper cause, as yet far from being conscious, knows not its own tendency. So is it with us, now skeptical, or without unity, because immersed in forms and effects all seeming to be of equal yet hostile value, and now religious, whilst in the reception of spiritual law. Bear with these distractions, with this coetaneous growth of the parts: they will one day be *members*, and obey one will. On that one will, on that secret cause, they nail our attention and hope. Life is hereby melted into an expectation or a religion. Underneath the inharmonious and trivial particulars, is a musical perfection, the Ideal journeying always with us, the heaven without rent or seam. Do but observe the mode of our illumination. When I converse with a profound mind, or if at any time being alone I have good thoughts, I do not at once arrive at satisfactions, as when, being thirsty, I drink water, or go to the fire, being cold: no! but I am at first apprised of my vicinity to a new and excellent region of life. By persisting to read or to think, this region gives further sign of itself, as it were in flashes of light, in sudden discoveries of its profound beauty and repose, as if the clouds that covered it parted at intervals, and showed the approaching traveller the inland mountains, with the tranquil eternal meadows spread at their base, whereon flocks graze, and shepherds pipe and dance. But every insight from this realm of thought is felt as initial, and promises a sequel. I do not make it; I arrive there, and behold what was there already. I make! O no! I clap my hands in infantine joy and amazement, before the first opening to me of this august magnificence, old with the love and homage of innumerable ages, young with the life of life, the sunbright Mecca of the desert. And what a future it opens! I feel a new heart beating with the love of the new beauty. I am ready to die out of nature, and be born again into this new yet unapproachable America I have found in the West.

> "Since neither now nor yesterday began
> These thoughts, which have been ever, nor yet can
> A man be found who their first entrance knew."

If I have described life as a flux of moods, I must now add, that there is that in us which changes not, and which ranks all sensations and states of mind. The consciousness in each man is a sliding scale, which identifies him now with the First Cause, and now with the flesh of his body; life above life, in infinite degrees. The sentiment from which it sprung determines the dignity of any deed, and the question ever is, not, what you have done or forborne, but, at whose command you have done or forborne it.

Fortune, Minerva, Muse, Holy Ghost,—these are quaint names, too narrow to cover this unbounded substance. The baffled intellect must still kneel before this cause, which refuses to be named,—ineffable cause, which every fine genius has essayed to represent by some emphatic symbol, as, Thales by water, Anaximenes by air, Anaxagoras by (*Nous*) thought, Zoroaster by fire, Jesus and the moderns by love: and the metaphor of each has become a national religion. The Chinese Mencius has not been the least successful in his generalization. "I fully understand language," he said, "and nourish well my vast-flowing vigor."—"I beg to ask what you call vast-flowing vigor?"—said his companion. "The explanation," replied Mencius, "is difficult. This vigor is supremely great, and in the highest degree unbending. Nourish it correctly, and do it no injury, and it will fill up the vacancy between heaven and earth. This vigor accords with and assists justice and reason, and leaves no hunger."—In our more correct writing, we give to this generalization the name of Being, and thereby confess that we have arrived as far as we can go. Suffice it for the joy of the universe, that we have not arrived at a wall, but at interminable oceans. Our life seems not present, so much as prospective; not for the affairs on which it is wasted, but as a hint of this vast-flowing vigor. Most of life seems to be mere advertisement of faculty: information is given us not to sell ourselves cheap; that we are very great. So, in particulars, our greatness is always in a tendency or direction, not in an action. It is for us to believe in the rule, not in the exception. The noble are thus known from the ignoble. So in accepting the leading of the sentiments, it is not what we believe concerning the immortality of the soul, or the like, but *the universal impulse to believe*, that is the material circumstance, and is the principal fact in the history of the globe. Shall we describe this cause as that which works directly? The spirit is not helpless or needful of mediate organs. It has plentiful powers and direct effects. I am explained without explaining, I am felt without acting, and where I am not. Therefore all just persons are satisfied with their own praise. They refuse to explain themselves, and are content that new actions should do them that office. They believe that we communicate without speech, and above speech, and that no right action of ours is quite unaffecting to our friends, at whatever distance; for the influence of action is not to be measured by miles. Why should I fret myself, because a circumstance has occurred, which hinders my presence where I was expected? If I am not at the meeting, my presence where I am, should be as useful to the commonwealth of friendship and wisdom, as would be my presence in that place. I exert the same quality of power in all places. Thus journeys the mighty Ideal before us; it never was known to fall into the rear. No man ever came to an experience which was satiating, but his good is tidings of a better. Onward and onward! In liberated moments, we know that a new picture of life and duty is already possible; the elements already exist in many minds around you, of a doctrine of life which shall transcend any written record we have. The new statement will comprise the skepticisms, as well as the faiths of society, and out of unbeliefs a creed shall be formed. For, skepticisms are not gratuitous or lawless, but are limitations of the affirmative statement, and the new philosophy must take them in, and make affirmations outside of them, just as much as it must include the oldest beliefs.

It is very unhappy, but too late to be helped, the discovery we have made, that we exist. That discovery is called the Fall of Man. Ever afterwards, we suspect our instruments. We have learned that we do not see directly, but mediately, and that we have no means of correcting these colored and distorting lenses which we are, or of computing the amount of their errors. Perhaps these subject-lenses have a creative power; perhaps there are no objects. Once we lived in what we saw; now, the rapaciousness of this new power, which threatens to absorb all things, engages us. Nature, art, persons, letters, religions,—objects, successively tumble in, and God is but one of its ideas. Nature and literature are subjective phenomena; every evil and every good thing is a shadow which we cast. The street is full of humiliations to the proud. As the fop contrived to dress his bailiffs in his livery, and make them wait on his guests at table, so the chagrins which the bad heart gives off as bubbles, at once take form as ladies and gentlemen in the street, shopmen or barkeepers in hotels, and threaten or insult whatever is threatenable and insultable in us. 'Tis the same with our idolatries. People forget that it is the eye which makes the horizon, and the rounding mind's eye which makes this or that man a type or representative of humanity with the name of hero or saint. Jesus the "providential man," is a good man on whom many people are agreed that these optical laws shall take effect. By love on one part, and by forbearance to press objection on the other part, it is for a time settled, that we will look at him in the centre of the horizon, and ascribe to him the properties that will attach to any man so seen. But the longest love or aversion has a speedy term. The great and crescive self, rooted in absolute nature, supplants all relative existence, and ruins the kingdom of mortal friendship and love. Marriage (in what is called the spiritual world) is impossible, because of the inequality between every subject and every object. The subject is the receiver of Godhead, and at every comparison must feel his being enhanced by that cryptic might. Though not in energy, yet by presence, this magazine of substance cannot be otherwise than felt: nor can any force of intellect attribute to the object the proper deity which sleeps or wakes forever in every subject. Never can love make consciousness and ascription equal in force. There will be the same gulf between every me and thee, as between the original and the picture. The universe is the bride of the soul. All private sympathy is partial. Two human beings are like globes, which can touch only in a point, and, whilst they remain in contact, all other points of each of the spheres are inert; their turn must also come, and the longer a particular union lasts, the more energy of appetency the parts not in union acquire.

Life will be imaged, but cannot be divided nor doubled. Any invasion of its unity would be chaos. The soul is not twin-born, but the only begotten, and though revealing itself as child in time, child in appearance, is of a fatal and universal power, admitting no co-life. Every day, every act betrays the ill-concealed deity. We believe in ourselves, as we do not believe in others. We permit all things to ourselves, and that which we call sin in others, is experiment for us. It is an instance of our faith in ourselves, that men never speak of crime as lightly as they think: or, every man thinks a latitude safe for himself, which is nowise to be indulged to another. The act looks very differently on the inside, and on the outside; in its quality, and in its consequences. Murder in the murderer is no such ruinous thought as poets and romancers will have it; it does not unsettle him, or fright him from his ordinary notice of trifles: it is an act quite easy to be contemplated, but in its sequel, it turns out to be a horrible jangle and confounding of all relations. Especially the crimes that spring from love, seem right and fair from the actor's point of view, but, when acted, are found destructive of society. No man at last believes that he can be lost, nor that the crime in him is as black as in the felon. Because the intellect qualifies in our own case the moral judgments. For there is no crime to the intellect. That is antinomian or hypernomian, and judges law as well as fact. "It is worse than a crime, it is a blunder," said Napoleon, speaking the language of the intellect. To it, the world is a problem in mathematics or the science of quantity, and it leaves out praise and blame, and all weak emotions. All stealing is comparative. If you come to absolutes, pray who does not steal? Saints are sad, because they behold sin, (even when they speculate,) from the point of view of the conscience, and not of the intellect; a confusion of thought. Sin seen from the thought, is a diminution or *less*: seen from the conscience or will, it is pravity or *bad*. The intellect names it shade, absence of light, and no essence. The conscience must feel it as essence, essential evil. This it is not: it has an objective existence, but no subjective.

Thus inevitably does the universe wear our color, and every object fall successively into the subject itself. The subject exists, the subject enlarges; all things sooner or later fall into place. As I am, so I see; use what language we will, we can never say anything but what we are; Hermes, Cadmus, Columbus, Newton, Buonaparte, are the mind's ministers. Instead of feeling a poverty when we encounter a great man, let us treat the new comer like a travelling geologist, who passes through our estate, and shows us good slate, or limestone, or anthracite, in our brush pasture. The partial action of each strong mind in one direction, is a telescope for the objects on which it is pointed. But every other part of knowledge is to be pushed to the same extravagance, ere the soul attains her due sphericity. Do you see that kitten chasing so prettily her own tail? If you could look with her eyes, you might see her surrounded with hundreds of figures performing complex dramas, with tragic and comic issues, long conversations, many characters, many ups and downs of fate,—and meantime it is only puss and her tail. How long before our masquerade will end its noise of tambourines, laughter, and shouting, and we shall find it was a solitary performance?—A subject and an object,—it takes so much to make the galvanic circuit complete, but magnitude adds nothing. What imports it whether it is Kepler and the sphere; Columbus and America; a reader and his book; or puss with her tail?

It is true that all the muses and love and religion hate these developments, and will find a way to punish the chemist, who publishes in the parlor the secrets of the laboratory. And we cannot say too little of our constitutional necessity of seeing things under private aspects, or saturated with our humors. And yet is the God the native of these bleak rocks. That need makes in morals the capital virtue of self-trust. We must hold hard to this poverty, however scandalous, and by more vigorous self-recoveries, after the sallies of action, possess our axis more firmly. The life of truth is cold, and so far mournful; but it is not the slave of tears, contritions, and perturbations. It does not attempt another's work, nor adopt another's facts. It is a main lesson of wisdom to know your own from another's. I have learned that I cannot dispose of other people's facts; but I possess such a key to my own, as persuades me against all their denials, that they also have a key to theirs. A sympathetic person is placed in the dilemma of a swimmer among drowning men, who all catch at him, and if he give so much as a leg or a finger, they will drown him. They wish to be saved from the mischiefs of their vices, but not from their vices. Charity would be wasted on this poor waiting on the symptoms. A wise and hardy physician will say, *Come out of that*, as the first condition of advice.

In this our talking America, we are ruined by our good nature and listening on all sides. This compliance takes away the power of being greatly useful. A man should not be able to look other than directly and forthright. A preoccupied attention is the only answer to the importunate frivolity of other people: an attention, and to an aim which makes their wants frivolous. This is a divine answer, and leaves no appeal, and no hard thoughts. In Flaxman's drawing of the Eumenides of Aeschylus, Orestes supplicates Apollo, whilst the Furies sleep on the threshold. The face of the god expresses a shade of regret and compassion, but calm with the conviction of the irreconcilableness of the two spheres. He is born into other politics, into the eternal and beautiful. The man at his feet asks for his interest in turmoils of the earth, into which his nature cannot enter. And the Eumenides there lying express pictorially this disparity. The god is surcharged with his divine destiny.

Illusion, Temperament, Succession, Surface, Surprise, Reality, Subjectiveness,—these are threads on the loom of time, these are the lords of life. I dare not assume to give their order, but I name them as I find them in my way. I know better than to claim any completeness for my picture. I am a fragment, and this is a fragment of me. I can very confidently announce one or another law, which throws itself into relief and form, but I am too young yet by some ages to compile a code. I gossip for my hour concerning the eternal politics. I have seen many fair pictures not in vain. A wonderful time I have lived in. I am not the novice I was fourteen, nor yet seven years ago. Let who will ask, where is the fruit? I find a private fruit sufficient. This is a fruit,—that I should not ask for a rash effect from meditations, counsels, and the hiving of truths. I should feel it pitiful to demand a result on this town and county, an overt effect on the instant month and year. The effect is deep and secular as the cause. It works on periods in which mortal lifetime is lost. All I know is reception; I am and I have: but I do not get, and when I have fancied I had gotten anything, I found I did not. I worship with wonder the great Fortune. My reception has been so large, that I am not annoyed by receiving this or that superabundantly. I say to the Genius, if he will pardon the proverb, *In for a mill, in for a million.* When I receive a new gift, I do not macerate my body to make the account square, for, if I should die, I could not make the account square. The benefit overran the merit the first day, and has overran the merit ever since. The merit itself, so-called, I reckon part of the receiving.

Also, that hankering after an overt or practical effect seems to me an apostasy. In good earnest, I am willing to spare this most unnecessary deal of doing. Life wears to me a visionary face. Hardest, roughest action is visionary also. It is but a choice betweens oft and turbulent dreams. People disparage knowing and the intellectual life, and urge doing. I am very content with knowing, if only I could know. That is an august entertainment, and would suffice me a great while. To know a little, would be worth the expense of this world. I hear always the law of Adrastia, "that every soul which had acquired any truth, should be safe from harm until another period."

I know that the world I converse with in the city and in the farms, is not the world I *think*. I observe that difference and shall observe it. One day, I shall know the value and law of this discrepance. But I have not found that much was gained by manipular attempts to realize the world of thought. Many eager persons successively make an experiment in this way, and make themselves ridiculous. They acquire democratic manners, they foam at the mouth, they hate and deny. Worse, I observe, that, in the history of mankind, there is never a solitary example of success,—taking their own tests of success. I say this polemically, or in reply to the inquiry, why not realize your world? But far be from me the despair which prejudges the law by a paltry empiricism,—since there never was a right endeavor, but it succeeded. Patience and patience, we shall win at the last. We must be very suspicious of the deceptions of the element of time. It takes a good deal of time to eat or to sleep, or to earn a hundred dollars, and a very little time to entertain a hope and an insight which becomes the light of our life. We dress our garden, eat our dinners, discuss the household with our wives, and these things make no impression, are forgotten next week; but in the solitude to which every man is always returning, he has a sanity and revelations, which in his passage into new worlds he will carry with him. Never mind the ridicule, never mind the defeat: up again, old heart!—it seems to say,—there is victory yet for all justice; and the true romance which the world exists to realize, will be the transformation of genius into practical power.

Selected Glossary of Terms used by Emerson

Art: the soul's action on the world; educates the perception of beauty.

Beauty: the underlying likenesses of the beautiful.

Behavior: my manner of life.

Body: my office, where I work.

Character: a reserved force which acts directly by presence; a latent power.

Civilization: the powers of a good woman.

Considerations: the positive centers of my actions.

Culture: my widest sympathies and affinities.

Dialectic: Platonic reasoning that drives through a subject to its essence.

Ethics: the soul illustrated in daily life.

Existence: the soul's need for an organ in nature.

Fate: the limitations of my inheritance and the natural world.

Freedom: state of being without any hindrance that does not arise out of my own constitution.

Generalization: a new influx of divinity into the mind.

History: the record of the works of the Universal Mind.

Illusions: the games and masks of my self-deception.

Instinct: revelations of the soul in the mind.

Intellect: the organ which sees an object as it stands in the light of science; cool and disengaged.

Intuition: An insight into the perfection of the laws of the soul.

Jesus: the mediator who instructs man to become like God. His purpose is to redeem us from a formal religion and to teach us to seek our well-being in the formation of the soul.

Literature: the soul's record in the world; a platform whence we may command a view of our present life; a purchase by which we may move it.

Logic: the procession or proportionate unfolding of the intuition.

Love of Truth: abstinence from dogmatism, recognition of the opposite negations between which the being is swung; respect for the highest law of being.

Man (human being): a stupendous antagonism, a dragging together of the poles of the universe; a god in ruins.

Manners: silent and mediate expressions of the soul.

Nature: an endless combination and repetition of a very few laws.

Obedience: the eye which reads the laws of the universe.

Organization: the mode in which the general soul incarnates itself in us.

Philosophy: the account which the human mind gives to itself of the constitution of the world.

Politics: the activity of the soul illustrated in power.

Power: my abilities and energies.

Purpose of the World: to realize the transformation of genius into practical power.

Religion: the emotion of reverence inspired by the soul.

Repose: synonymous with ignorance. God offers to every mind its choice between truth and repose.

Science: the discovery of the soul's methods.

Soul: not an organ but what animates the organs; not a function but what uses function; not a faculty but a light; not intellect or will but the master of the intellect and the will. It is related to the world.

Teaching: he who gives, and he who receives. There is no teaching until the pupil is brought into the same state or principle as the teacher; a transfusion takes place; the teacher is the pupil and the pupil is the teacher; then is a teaching.

Thinking: a pious reception.

Trades: the learning of the soul in nature by labor.

Transcendentalism: intuitive thought; also, Idealism.

Virtue: the adherence in action to the nature of things; a perpetual substitution of being for seeming.

Wealth: my gains and losses.

Wisdom: To finish the moment, to find the journey's end in every step of the road; to live the greatest number of good hours.

Worship: my belief.

Index